BUILDING
WEALTH FOR
BUILDING THE
KINGDOM

BUILDING
WEALTH FOR
BUILDING THE
KINGDOM

A Financial Planning Guide for Latter-day Saint Families

2012 Edition

DEVIN D. THORPE

Building Wealth for Building the Kingdom: A Financial Planning Guide for Latter-day Saint Families 2012 Edition

ISBN: 1470096199

ISBN-13: 978-1470096199

TABLE OF CONTENTS

ACKNOWLEDGEMENTS 9

DISCLAIMER 11

ABOUT THE AUTHOR. 13

CHAPTER 1 : INTRODUCTION 15

CHAPTER 2 : OPTIMIZING INCOME 19

CHAPTER 3 : DEVELOPING A PLAN 27

CHAPTER 4 : TITHING 35

CHAPTER 5 : MANAGING DEBT 43

CHAPTER 6 : OWNING A CAR (or small fleet) 55

CHAPTER 7 : OWNING A HOME 65

CHAPTER 8 : FINANCING MISSIONS 75

CHAPTER 9 : FINANCING EDUCATION 81

CHAPTER 10 : INSURANCE 89

CHAPTER 11 : RETIREMENT 97

CHAPTER 12 : TAXES 105

CHAPTER 13 : YOUR PERSONAL FINANCIAL PLAN 111

CHAPTER 14 : INVESTMENT ALTERNATIVES 119

CHAPTER 15 : INVESTMENT ACCOUNTS 129

CHAPTER 16 : MEASURING SUCCESS 137

NOTE FROM THE AUTHOR 141

For Gail, without whom, I would have no money.

ACKNOWLEDGEMENTS

HAVING WORKED ON this book off and on for fifteen years, it is almost impossible to remember all of the people who have contributed to this effort. To any I've forgotten, I sincerely apologize. I am particularly grateful to friends who read early drafts and contributed valuable ideas for making the book better. Among those, I am especially grateful to are Michael Benson, Jim Christensen, Mitch Walkington and Cindy England, each of whom gave me great suggestions for improving the book. I owe a special debt of gratitude to John T. Child (johntchild.com) for the beautiful cover design. Natalie T. Child proved to be an impeccable proof reader who served to correct countless errors that had previously escaped me.

The person who has contributed the most, however, is my wife, Gail, who has read multiple drafts, providing encouragement along the way and giving me the space (in every conceivable dimension) required to get this done.

Notwithstanding their great contributions, let me point out that any errors that remain in this book are my responsibility.

DISCLAIMER

NEITHER THE AUTHOR nor any other person associated with this book may be held liable for any damages that may result from following the counsel in this book. No single book of financial advice can be used as a substitute for professional, personalized financial advice. Readers are encouraged to seek financial advice from qualified professionals, including licensed investment advisors, stockbrokers, accountants, insurance agents, attorneys and other qualified individuals.

ABOUT THE AUTHOR

DEVIN D. THORPE brings a broad perspective to financial planning, having owned and operated an investment-banking firm—which included an investment advisory business—a mortgage brokerage and having served in a variety of corporate finance positions.

Presently, Devin serves as a business professor at South China University of Technology in Guangzhou, China on behalf of Brigham Young University's Kennedy Center China Teachers program. Previously, he served as the Chief Financial Officer for the multinational company MonaVie, listed in Inc. Magazine's 2009 Inc. 500 as the 18th fastest growing company in America and, at $834 million in revenue, the third largest company on the list. Prior experience includes two years working on the staff of the U.S. Senate Banking Committee during Utah Senator Jake Garn's tenure. He also served briefly in Utah State Government, working at USTAR under Governor Jon Huntsman.

He earned an MBA with focus in Finance and Accounting from Cornell University's Johnson Graduate School of Management. He completed his undergraduate degree in finance at the University of Utah, where he later worked as an adjunct professor of finance. In 2006, Devin was recognized by the David Eccles School of Business at the University of Utah as a Distinguished Alum.

In the Church, Devin presently serves as a seminary teacher along with his wife, Gail. Previously, he served as a counselor in a stake presidency, a counselor in a bishopric, ward executive secretary, young men's president, assistant scout master, three times as an assistant ward clerk, and in more elders quorum presidencies than he can count.

Devin ran his first marathon in 2011, finishing in 4:35.

You can reach Devin via email at devin@devinthorpe.com.

CHAPTER 1

INTRODUCTION

But before ye seek for riches, seek ye for the kingdom of God.

And after ye have obtained a hope in Christ ye shall obtain riches, if ye seek them; and ye will seek them for the intent to do good—to clothe the naked, and to feed the hungry, and to liberate the captive, and administer relief to the sick and the afflicted.

— Jacob 2:18-19

LDS Motivation

THIS BOOK HAS been written for those Latter-day Saints (members of the Church of Jesus Christ of Latter-day Saints) who believe that it is more important to do good than to do well. That is to say, it is written for you because you believe it is more important to raise a good family, attend to your Church duties, send your children on missions and pay tithing than it is for you to accumulate wealth. You may, therefore, lack adequate financial planning. The objective of this book is to help you to prepare financially to render any service that you may be called to give.

Brigham Young best expressed what has become the theme for this book. He said, "If, by industrious habits and honorable dealings, you obtain thousands or millions, little or much, it is your duty to use all that is put in your possession, as judiciously as you have knowledge, to build up the Kingdom of God on the earth."[1]

What Brigham Young suggests is something akin to consecration. The Church does not now require that we currently share all of our wealth directly with the Church or that we keep all things in common. Instead, we live a preparatory law of tithing and the payment of offerings. Beyond that, we give to the Church much of our free time. We save and invest our money to prepare our children to enter life as contributing members of the Church. We save and invest to send our children on missions and to serve missions ourselves.

This preparatory law is good preparation for living the higher law. So much of our time, talents and resources are already dedicated directly to building the kingdom that to go to the next step of fully consecrating our assets and income to the Lord should become relatively simple. It is not inappropriate to consider financial planning from the standpoint of preparing ourselves for living this higher law.

Self-reliance is a fundamental precept of our Latter-day religion. President Hinckley explained this concept in an interview with the BBC in 1995, saying:

> We teach emphatically the importance of self-reliance, the importance of education, of equipping our people so they can earn a living; the importance of saving and being prudent in the management of their affairs; the importance of setting something aside, a reserve, to take care of their needs if there should come a rainy day in their lives. And it's amazing how many follow that teaching. That's basic with us.[2]

This desire for self-reliance, therefore, further defines who we are as Latter-day Saints and how we approach the task of financial planning. Our objective, therefore, is to be able to provide for ourselves and our family members all of the things we desire them to have—without reliance upon a government dole or help from the Church.

Although you may never have thought about it before, your perspective on financial planning is likely somewhat different than other people's. The motivations you may have as a Latter-day Saint in accumulating wealth are likely associated with a desire to render service to others, to build up the Lord's Kingdom, to prepare yourself to live the law of consecration and, finally, a desire to be self-reliant.

---

1   *Discourses of Brigham Young*, pp. 313-314.
2   Gordon B. Hinckley, *Teachings of Gordon B. Hinckley*, Deseret Book, 1997, p. 586.

LDS Issues

Latter-day Saints face financial challenges different from other groups of people. Our financial planning issues are different due to an identifiable set of issues that distinguish us from other people.

Tithing is not uniquely an LDS doctrine, but few other religionists practice a ten percent tithe with the commitment of the Latter-day Saints. The Saints practice the law of tithing with enthusiasm that may result in part from relief at not being asked to practice the higher law of consecration.

Latter-day Saints are recognized as having large families. Having adopted the Lord's admonition to "be fruitful, multiply and replenish the Earth,"[3] given to Adam and Eve as being a relevant command in 2012, the Saints do have larger families, on average, than other Americans. The number of children we have creates a financial planning challenge—particularly as respects education.

Missions, not only for our young men, but also for our daughters and ourselves, create a distinction in our financial planning from financial planning for those of other faiths. Missions are, perhaps, one of the easiest financial objectives for which we can prepare if we start the process early. Missions as couples in retirement needn't require substantial wealth, but planning and preparation are nonetheless important.

After considering all of the peculiar financial planning aspects of Latter-day Saints, it is also important to put the traditional issues of education, home ownership, retirement, etc. into an LDS context.

While Latter-day Saints do have a significant set of financial planning issues in common, each family will have a different set of particulars. It is important, therefore, to seek the advice of competent advisors (this may not be your brother-in-law). Such advisors should include a CPA to advise you on tax planning issues, insurance agents to help you with both life insurance and casualty insurance policies, a stockbroker and or a financial planner to help you with your investments. Remember, however, that this is your money. You should be making the decisions based upon your best judgment after gathering information from all appropriate sources. Until and unless you approach an age or condition where you, or others, question your competence to make such decisions, you should take responsibility. Remember, your stockbroker doesn't have to live off of your investments, but eventually you will.

---

[3]   Genesis 1:28

Book Structure and Outline

As you read this book, it will be helpful for you to understand the organization of the book. Each chapter will provide a discussion of an element of your financial plan from tithing to taxes and from missions to education. The focus of the book will be on the practical steps that you will need to undertake to have a successful financial plan.

At the end of each chapter, you will find a short list of action items that summarize or distill the discussion to a set of simple tasks. These tasks, from chapter to chapter, will overlap and repeat occasionally. Consider each to be a reminder of the actions you should be taking to maximize your financial plan.

Action Items:

1. Read the book.
2. Apply the concepts to your particular circumstance.
3. Identify advisors who can help you put the concepts into action.

CHAPTER 2

OPTIMIZING INCOME

If we will work unitedly, we can work ourselves into wealth, health, prosperity and power, and this is required of us. It is the duty of a Saint of God to gain all the influence he can on this Earth, and to use every particle of that influence to do good.

— *Discourses of Brigham Young, Pg.285*

What is meant by "optimizing income?"

IN THE FIRST draft of this text, this chapter was titled "Maximizing Income." You can understand why, of course. The more income, the better, right? Wrong.

Hence the revised title, "Optimizing Income."

For every household, tax situation and family circumstance there is an optimal level of income that is likely something less than the theoretical maximum level of income achievable.

At the extreme, you would certainly agree that sending a six-year-old into coal mines for ten hours per day in order to add $10 per month to your household income would be sub-optimal. The same may be true for many other efforts at maximizing household income.

Provider: The primary breadwinner in the family should appropriately focus on developing a successful career. It matters little whether this is a blue-collar trade or a white-collar profession, the family provider should be focused on advancing that career through the accumulation of additional relevant skills, certifications, education, etc. In some careers, i.e., education, law, public accounting, such continuing education or re-certification is required for licensing.

Even if continuing education requirements are not imposed in your chosen career, it is a good idea to read up on your chosen field; stay current with the industries best practices so that you are always at the top of your game.

This suggests that alternate pursuits that are undertaken purely for the sake of the revenue generated should be minimized. If you are moonlighting to make ends meet, you probably can't stay late at your career position to put in the extra effort to finish a job on time or prepare for the next day's work. So, for the sake of a few extra dollars of current income, you may be sacrificing long-term career potential.

If the motivation for your moonlighting is to sustain a particular lifestyle, you'd have to agree that the irony is pretty thick. How can you enjoy a lifestyle that requires you to work 60 or more hours per week at two jobs? If your motivation is to accumulate wealth for the sake of doing good, consider that you are giving up opportunities to serve in the Church now. Can you effectively serve in a calling that requires a significant amount of time if you are always exhausted from your work? If your motivation is to provide for your family, you may want to ask them in a sincere, prayerful family council if they wouldn't prefer for you to earn less to be at home more.

All of that said, some people engage in activities that generate money on the side, but the primary motivation is not the revenue they generate but the pleasure derived from the activity. Everyone should have a hobby—an outside interest to provide diversion from the stress of the routine. If your hobby generates a bit of income, perhaps only to fund the cost of participation in the hobby, fantastic! Financially, it certainly beats having an expensive hobby from which you can derive no income.

Second Income: In many homes today, both parents work because they believe that there is no alternative. It may be hard to believe, however, that in many cases, work outside the home contributes so little to the family budget that if the facts were presented clearly, the secondary income earner in your family would quit work in a heartbeat.

Let's consider a for instance. If the primary breadwinner earns $70,000 and the secondary breadwinner earns $30,000 per year, you'd be inclined to think that the second income contributes 30% of the net household income. Nope. Due to the U.S. tax structure, the second income may contribute less than 14% of the disposable income of the family. The secondary income in a marriage is taxed at the same rate as if one person earned all the money—it is taxed, therefore at the marginal rate—which is a higher effective rate than the primary provider is paying. In certain circumstances, two married people in the U.S. who both work will pay *even more* in total taxes than a similar household where one spouse makes as much as the two combined incomes in the first (this happens when the one income exceeds the social security tax "wage base limit").

The first dollars earned in the home are effectively exempt from income tax. You receive a standard deduction or mortgage interest deduction and exemptions for each member of the family. The next dollars are taxed at the lowest rate, 10%. This rate applies to the first $17,000 of taxable income for married couples filing jointly for 2011. The next layer of income is taxed at 15%. The marginal rates continue to rise up to 39%. All of this income is also subject to Social Security and Medicare Taxes. (Note that a household with one income of $150,000 will typically pay less social security tax than a household with two incomes totaling $150,000.)

Add to these taxes, state taxes—which vary widely from no income tax to rates that approach half the Federal level.

Please note that if you go check the tax withholdings from your paychecks, you may not see these proportions borne out. In fact, however, when you file your tax return at the end of each year, the formulas work in this way.

Finally, you have committed to pay ten percent of your income in tithing. Calculated on the gross wages, for sake of this example, you can begin to see the tremendous tax burden associated with marginal income.

Now consider whether or not there are any expenses in your home associated directly with having a spouse work outside the home. There are a number of small expenses such as more dinners out, laundry services and perhaps housecleaning. Of greater financial import would be childcare and automobiles. If you own a second or third car primarily because of the second income earner's commute, there may be literally nothing left after covering all of the taxes, tithing and direct expenses associated with outside employment.

Consider the analysis in the following table based on 2011 tax rates.

Secondary Income Analysis	With Secondary Income	Without Secondary Income	Benefit/ (Loss) from Secondary Income
Income			
Income from Primary Provider	$70,000	$70,000	
Income from Secondary Provider	$30,000		$30,000
Total Income:	$100,000	$70,000	$30,000
Taxes			
Payroll Taxes*	$5,650	$3,955	$(1,695)
Federal Income Taxes**	$13,500	$7,400	$(6,100)
State Income Taxes***	$4,250	$2,750	$(1,500)
Federal Tax Benefit of State Taxes	$(1,063)	$(413)	$650
Total Taxes	$22,338	$13,693	$(8,645)
After Tax Income	$77,663	$56,308	$21,355
Donations			
Tithing	$10,000	$7,000	$3,000
Tax Benefit of Tithing	$(2,500)	$(1,050)	$(1,450)
Net effect of tithing	$7,500	$5,950	$1,550
After Tax and Tithing Income	$70,163	$50,358	$19,805
Direct Expenses of Second Income			
Car	$6,000		$6,000
Childcare	$3,600		$3,600
Misc.	$2,000		$2,000
Total Direct Expenses of Second Income	$11,600		$11,600
Income after Tax, Tithing and Direct Expenses	$58,563	$50,358	$8,205

* For 2011 the payroll tax for Social Security was temporarily cut to 4.2%; Medicare taxes of 1.45% were not reduced.

** Assumes $15,000 of fixed exemptions and deductions.

*** Varies by state.

In this example, the secondary income of $30,000 contributes just $8,205 after taxes, tithing and direct expenses associated with employment. Every situation is different. At the extreme, a secondary income can actually be a drain on the family budget. For instance, $6,000 (used above) represents the cost of ownership for a very inexpensive car; the cost of ownership for a large sport utility vehicle would be more than twice that amount.

On the other hand, if your total household income is below $80,000 or if you have lots of children, the tax penalty for a second income is not as high. If no daycare costs are required because of a generous grandparent or because there are no children in the home who require care, more of the income can drop to the bottom line. If you need to have a second income in your home, see if you can find a position that will allow you to travel via public transit or in a car pool so that you don't need to purchase a second car just to provide a second income.

You should also consider the impact of the secondary income on the family. If both providers are eagerly pursuing intrinsically rewarding careers and there is no adverse impact on the family, it may be of little import how much (or how little) is generated by the secondary income. On the other hand, if the secondary income earner prefers not to work and there is a negative impact on the well being of the family, it may not matter how much is generated by the secondary income.

Before you make a dramatic change in your lifestyle like having a breadwinner quit or selling a car, it makes good sense to consult with a tax advisor or financial planner who can help you to evaluate your particular financial circumstance.

Children: Your children will also need to learn the value of a dollar and the importance of hard work. You can begin this process by providing them with an allowance—a portion of which is tied to performance of household chores. How much to pay your children will depend upon your circumstances and, to some extent, on the allowance that the other children in the neighborhood receive.

As they get older, children can be encouraged to earn some income outside the home. Until they do, no matter how well your kids learn to manage the money you provide, they're still spending your money. And they haven't learned to provide for themselves or to be somewhat self-reliant. Children and teenagers need to have a balanced life. For most, however, there is room for a part-time job that won't interfere with school, athletics or Church activities.

Keep the Sabbath Day Holy

There is a special class of income to be avoided by Latter-day Saints. This would be income generated through any violation of the Sabbath. We now live in a world that operates 24 hours per day, seven days per week. There is virtually no business that does not require some of its employees to work on the Sabbath. Furthermore, there are noble tasks that must be completed even on the Sabbath. The sick and elderly still need care; milk cows must be milked, and those who are employed in a public safety capacity must often take their turns on the Sabbath. That said, many of us do have a choice whether to work on the Sabbath.

Brigham Young, in his forthright way, expressed his feelings about the Sabbath as follows:

> Now remember, my brethren, those who go skating, buggy riding or on excursions on the Sabbath day—and there is a great deal of this practised [sic]—are weak in the faith. Generally, little by little, the spirit of their religion leaks out of their hearts and their affections, and by and by they begin to see fault in their brethren, faults in the doctrines of the Church, faults in the organization, and at last they leave the Kingdom of God and go to destruction. The Lord has directed his people to rest one-seventh part of the time, and we take the first day of the week, and call it our Sabbath. This is according to the order of the Christians. We should observe this for our own temporal good and spiritual welfare. When we see a farmer in a hurry, that he has to attend to his harvest, and to haying, fencemaking, or to gathering his cattle on the Sabbath day, as far as I am concerned, I count him weak in the faith. He has lost the spirit of his religion, more or less. Six days are enough for us to work, and if we wish to play, play within the six days; if we wish to go on excursions, take one of those six days, but on the seventh day, come to the place of worship, attend to the Sacrament, confess your faults one to another and to our God, and pay attention to the ordinances of the house of God. [4]

Maximize Your Net

Whenever cash runs short, there are two temptations that may enter your mind. The first thought is frequently to say, "I'll make more money

---

[4]   *Discourses of Brigham Young*, p. 165.

next _____ (week, month, year) and then I can afford to pay back the money I borrow today." This practice of spending your next raise has been called spending "if-come." It leads to unmanageable levels of debt and associated misery. See chapter five for a complete discussion of managing debt.

The second temptation that arises is a desire to go out and "make some quick money" to solve the problem. As we've discussed, many such efforts are short sighted and ineffective. Consider that $100 of marginal income may be worth just $51 after taxes and tithing, depending upon your marginal tax rate. On the other hand, if you can reduce your spending by $100 you really save $100. This is because you are spending after-tax dollars but you generate dollars that have yet to be taxed.

This makes it much more difficult to solve your budget problems by perpetually trying to earn more money. Part of the problem is the mindset. If you believe that you can create wealth by earning more money, you may find that you spend it as fast—or faster—than you generate your income. There is nothing easier to do than to spend the money you make.

The surest way to have money in the bank tomorrow is to put it there today. After a time, your savings start to generate an income that becomes material. Before you retire, for instance, your retirement savings should be generating nearly as much income for reinvestment as you earn with a salary. In fact, that is one way to measure whether you are ready to retire. If your investments generate as much income as you can by working, you are probably close to being ready for retirement (more on that in chapter 11).

The concept of before vs. after-tax dollars also suggests that there is greater value than you previously believed in the things you do for yourself that you would otherwise pay someone to do for you. For instance, if you pay someone $100 per month to clean your home, you really need to earn almost $200 to generate enough income to cover that expense. If you pay $100 per month to have your shirts laundered, you need to generate $200 per month to cover that expense.

Food storage can provide an opportunity to reduce your long-term food bill. By buying in bulk, you can reduce your per-unit cost of buying food. Furthermore, if you can raise some food in your garden, every dollar you save reduces your need to generate income by almost $2 dollars.

The bottom line is that if you want your bottom line to grow, focus more on the expenses you can eliminate than on your strategies to expand your top-line income.

Action Items:

1. Develop your career by emphasizing training, education and dedication to your primary career.

2. Carefully evaluate the costs and benefits associated with any secondary income sources in your home.

3. Teach your children the value of money and the benefits of self-reliance.

4. Remember that frugality is generally worth more to your bottom line than increases in income.

CHAPTER 3

DEVELOPING A PLAN

Would you like to know how [to become rich]? I can tell you in a very few words — never want a thing you cannot get, live within your means, manufacture that which you wear, and raise that which you eat.

— Discourses of Brigham Young, Pg.180 - Pg.181.

Feel Wealthy by Wanting Less

T-SHIRTS RARELY OFFER genuine insights, but a popular message seen in Maui reads "There are two ways to become rich: make more or want less." It is our nature to want more, but it is easier to want less. In truth, the more powerful financial principal is, as Brigham Young put it, "never want a thing you cannot get."

Much of what many people aspire to own represents not a practical necessity or good investment, but presumed evidence of wealth or trappings of affluence. Such items—whether they be fashions, cars, boats or whatever other asset that signals to the neighbors a certain level of wealth—are poor investments. Too often, these are purchased with credit cards or other loans. As a result, unforgiving debt is incurred in order to own depreciating assets, some of which require expensive insurance, maintenance, storage and care. Such elaborate toys can also be a distraction from church and family duties.

In contrast, if the funds used to purchase, support and maintain an affluent lifestyle were instead invested in appreciating assets, over time a true level of affluence can be created. Financial independence can be achieved and time allowed for family and church service.

An appropriate guideline for determining whether or not such purchases will represent an inappropriate financial burden would simply be whether or not you can make the purchase from cash—not borrowing—without interrupting your overall financial plan.

Therefore, the first key to financial planning is to want fewer of the trappings of affluence.

Develop a Plan to Achieve Financial Goals

It is imperative to plan for your future. This book will help you to calculate the current monthly rate for debt elimination, home and car purchases and saving for your retirement and your children's missions and education. For most people, it will never be easier to start saving for these expenses than it is right now.

Today, time is on your side. Whether your missionary will be leaving in six months or six years, you are much better off to start planning and saving today rather than to wait. By starting to save for a mission just two years before a missionary leaves, you can cut the monthly cost by more than half. By starting when your missionary is baptized at age eight, you can cut the monthly cost to a mere fraction of what it will cost to fund the mission from your income and cash flow while he or she is gone.

There are two reasons why time can be so helpful. First, everything you put into savings this month will grow (if properly invested) until the time comes that you need it. The other advantage of starting early is simply that there are more paychecks between now and then—whatever that event is. If you are planning for retirement, it will be easier to develop a comfortable plan in your thirties than in your fifties—you'll have three times as many paychecks from which to deduct a small amount for investing.

Deferring the benefits of your earned income takes some discipline. It is easy to feel as though spending money provides joy. Properly done, saving money can also provide joy. You'll find, if you haven't already, that when you start to save you achieve a sense of accomplishment precisely because it is difficult. Every month you can draw closer to your ultimate financial objectives. In order to be successful, however, most people need to go through the steps to create a clear financial plan, including a monthly budget.

Keep a Cushion

One of the objectives of developing a budget is to create savings for various events, i.e., missions, education, retirement, etc. Each such event should have a dedicated pool of funds. The easiest way to accomplish this is to have separate savings accounts for each purpose. One special account that will not be covered elsewhere in this book, is a cushion account.

The cushion account (or possibly accounts) should have two layers. One layer will be what you use for major purchases; the other, virtually untouchable layer, is for emergencies. You'll contribute a planned amount to the account every month (you set the amount). Then, when the account exceeds the emergency balance, you can start using the surplus balances for major purchases.

This top layer is how you pay for a new piece of furniture or a new appliance—not with credit. It is a sad irony that many people find it easier to spend borrowed money than to spend savings, even though the borrowed money is more costly. The interest costs are higher, the risk to your financial health are higher and yet, likely because it is someone else's money, many people find it easier to spend. Don't you be one of them. If it is difficult to spend money that it takes you years to accrue, that's the whole idea.

A new washer and dryer won't earn interest, won't send your children on missions and won't pay for your retirement—only cash in the bank can help you with that.

Now, you'll need to develop an emergency layer in your accounts. Experts disagree about how much money you should have as an emergency reserve. The truth is, it depends upon your situation and the nature of the emergency—which sadly cannot be predicted.

The most likely emergency will be a temporary loss of income. The most likely cause of this for most folks is temporary unemployment. The likely period of unemployment is one month for every $10,000 of annual income earned. So, if you earn $30,000 per year, your cushion should cover three months.

You needn't cover tithing and taxes in the emergency fund because without income, those items won't occur. You'll also not need to cover savings contributions in your emergency fund. During a short gap in your cash flow, it would be inappropriate to continue to contribute to savings—you'd just be moving money from one account to another. Finally, there are some discretionary expenses that you could eliminate from spending during such a time. If you have good food storage, your food bill can also be substantially reduced.

The bottom line, therefore, is that you'll need to cover only your debts and other fixed obligations such as utilities, insurance, etc. This may mean that you'll only need to have half of your income for the period you estimated above in savings. Be sure to calculate your target carefully.

Don't look to credit for your emergency fund, either. Your creditors may have the option of rescinding your credit if anything should happen to your financial status to cause them concern.

Don't think of your mission funds, education funds, retirement or other long-term savings accounts as your emergency funds. As soon as you can, develop your two-layer cushion so that your long-term financial objectives are not jeopardized by the possibility of a short-term financial crisis.

How to Plan

A good financial plan consists of three key steps: preparing, enforcing and measuring. It will do you little good, for instance, to have an elaborate plan worked out on paper, if it is never enforced and if progress is never measured.

Prepare the Plan

Your plan needs to cover not only the expenses that you routinely incur, but also the savings commitments that you may not have been making. In order to include all of the savings that you'll want in your budget, you'll need to finish reading this book. Chapter 13 includes a worksheet that will help you bring your whole financial plan into perspective.

The first thing in your plan will be tithing. Then savings will be added. Taxes and insurance costs will be factored in. Your debt service (the total of all your monthly debt payments) can then be calculated. A special category for your car purchase will be included, as well. Finally, you'll need to add in a detailed plan for your spending—a detailed budget.

After you have factored in all of the above, you may be tempted to simply allocate the balance to your other expenses. If you do this without regard to what you've been spending, you'll find either that you are miserable or that you aren't living within your budget. Therefore, start by looking at your actual expenses for as far back as you can stand to do it— at least a month, but shoot for a full year. This will ensure that you capture all of your seasonal expenses, like Christmas, first day of school, or summer vacations. If you build a budget without any of these items, you are likely to blow the budget.

When you are done with your budget, you should have your total monthly gross income at the top and a list of commitments and expenses—including savings and taxes—that total the same amount.

There are some wonderful tools available for budgeting. For those who are computer oriented, Microsoft Money and Quicken offer powerful financial management packages that help you plan, measure and even enforce your budget. For those who prefer non-electronic means of budgeting, there is no better system than the *Rich on Any Income* budgeting system.

Rich on Any Income

Financial planners Jim Christensen and Clint Coombs wrote the definitive budget book, *Rich on Any Income*; it was published by Deseret Book in 1985.

The brilliance of their budgeting book is the system they invented. Using a checkbook-sized budget booklet, they brought the final two steps—enforcement and measurement—of budgeting together at the time of the expenditure.

Using their simple system, you allocate your current checkbook balance, less any credit card balances outstanding, to your budget categories. Then each paycheck you add more to each category. With each expenditure, you write down the item in your checkbook—even if it is a credit card transaction—and then you deduct the same amount from the budget category. Hence, you always know—up to the minute—how much money is available for spending in any category. Enforcement and measurement cannot be brought any closer to the purchase decision point than this system provides.

Each month, you start a new booklet by bringing the balances forward from the old booklet. The booklets can be easily produced at home and the system is easy to follow. The time spent on the process is distributed across the month—a few seconds at each transaction.

Enforce the Plan

While this certainly sounds harsh, the implication should be that you are taking control of your finances so that they don't control you. Without this element of self-discipline incorporated into your budget process, you cannot accomplish your long-term objectives. There will always be something that chips away at the plan—it takes some courage to fight these temptations.

There is a trick that may help you to be more in control. First, make sure that you make your tithing payments, savings contributions and debt payments as soon as you get your money. Better yet, have these amounts automatically transferred, where possible, from your checking account so that you have no choice in making these payments. This will leave you with only your discretionary budget cash in the checking account. Now, all you have to do is to live within the constraints of the available cash. This reduces the need to catch up the budget entries every day—all you have to do is keep track of your checking account balance and reconcile it monthly.

Measure the Plan

Periodically, whether daily, weekly or monthly, you need to measure your progress. The more frequently you undertake to measure your progress, the more control you'll enjoy. There are two aspects that need to be measured: first, income and expenses and, second, asset and liability balances.

Each month, you'll want to measure your income and expenses and compare them to your budget. Your personal "income statement" is really no different than that of a business; you need to earn more than you spend. It is this process of spending less than you make every month that allows you to steadily accumulate a strong balance sheet.

At least quarterly, you'll want to measure your balance sheet compared to your last balance sheet. Your balance sheet consists of a list of all of your assets, including cash accounts, investment accounts, your home, cars and other valuable assets. Though many people include personal assets—clothes and furniture—in their balance sheet, it would be more conservative to exclude these items. Do you really want to sell them in a pinch? Probably not. And how much are your used socks going to fetch at a garage sale?

The other side of the balance sheet is your liabilities. These represent the amounts you owe, including your mortgage, car loans, student loans and credit cards. If you have unpaid taxes or tithing, be sure to include these items as liabilities as well.

Your net worth represents the value of your assets minus the sum of your liabilities. Focus on improving your net worth. Every time you go through this exercise you should see that the difference improves—assets should increase and liabilities should decline.

Another layer of sophistication in this regard, would be to identify the purpose of each investment account and compare the current balance to the target balance. This book can help you identify target balances for missions, education and retirement. Check your progress whenever you prepare a balance sheet.

If you keep your budget on a computerized system, you'll find it easy to run these reports and measure your progress.

Action Items:

1. Want fewer of the trappings of affluence.
2. Plan for the future.
3. Develop a budget.
4. Live within your budget.
5. Measure your progress toward your long-term goals.

CHAPTER 4

TITHING

Bring ye all the tithes into the storehouse, that there may be meat in mine house, and prove me now herewith, saith the LORD of hosts, if I will not open you the windows of heaven, and pour you out a blessing, that *there shall not be room* enough *to receive it.*

— *Malachi 3:10*

Prove Me Now Herewith

A WEALTHY STAKE PRESIDENT was reportedly asked by a poor widow in his stake how he achieved financial success. He replied without a thought, "I've always paid my tithing."

Her quiet—and likely unheard—retort, "I, too, have always paid mine," raises the question of just how one accepts the Lord's challenge to "prove [Him] now herewith."

This simple story suggests that wealth is either not the measure of the proof the Lord intended or that the challenge is more complex than simply paying tithing.

It would be unfair to suggest that this widow, or other people, who have paid their tithing but have not accumulated wealth are undeserving or that the Lord hasn't blessed them—certainly they are worthy and He has undeniably blessed them in other ways.

If your objective in accepting the Lord's challenge, however, is to accumulate sufficient means to not only provide for your family but also to provide for lifelong, active church service, there is likely more to the Lord's challenge than merely paying tithing and waiting for the windows of heaven to open and rain prosperity upon you. Malachi's record may subtly hint at the issue—"there shall not be room enough to receive it."

Imagine that 401(k) plans, IRA's, mutual funds, are buckets to catch the Lord's blessings from heaven and that a disciplined spending plan is a funnel to get the blessings into the buckets. This is how we make "room enough" to receive some of the Lord's blessings.

Making Room

Of course you wouldn't expect the Lord to be accruing a secret pension for someone that hasn't been saving as she should or to create a mission fund for a teenager who invests all of his income in his "awesome" music collection for his iPod.

Clearly, then, it behooves us to do more than pay tithing and wait for blessings. As with all laws, the Lord has made clear that He understands the laws of finance. Various parables in the New Testament suggest the importance of financial stewardship. While these references are frequently used as allegories for spiritual matters, they nonetheless provide evidence of financial savvy on the Lord's part. We shouldn't expect the Creator of heaven and earth to be as perplexed by the time value of money as most of us are.

The nominal point of one such parable in Matthew 25:14-30 (the Kingdom of Heaven as a man travelling into a far country) was that the wise steward who earned the greatest financial return on his talents or capital was given the talents of the "wicked and slothful servant." The Lord went so far as to suggest a specific investment strategy to the disappointed servant, "Thou oughtest therefore to have put my money to the exchangers," as that would have provided a favorable return.

The Lord expects us to learn and employ the basic laws of personal financial planning. He won't develop your spending plan for you. He will, however, help you develop the self-discipline to use it. He won't walk to the bank to open an IRA for you. He will, however, help you to have the courage to defer current spending in order to make a current investment.

This book will provide you, with a basic understanding of personal financial planning principles; to really put the Lord to the test and make room for the blessings He'll pour out upon you, you may wish to obtain substantially greater knowledge. The more you know and understand about money and investing the more room you'll be able to provide the Lord for His blessings.

Do Your Part

In addition to learning and abiding the basic principles of personal finance, the Lord requires that we be anxiously engaged in the process of generating sufficient income for our needs. As with financial planning, you would not expect the Lord to bless a slothful employee to keep his job if he called in sick every day and then went skiing—even if he had paid his tithing.

Joseph Fielding Smith articulated our responsibility to "be industrious" in terms that remain crystal clear almost 100 years after he first spoke them.

> All men and women should feel a degree of independence of character that would stimulate them to do something for a living, and not be idle; for it is written that the idler shall not eat the bread of the laborer of Zion, and he shall not have place among us. Therefore, it is necessary that we should be industrious, that we should intelligently apply our labor to something that is productive and conducive to the welfare of the human family.[5]

In the Prophet's mind, clearly, idlers were not entitled to the blessings of tithing, including particularly, direct assistance from the Church. It is a logical conclusion, therefore, that the Lord feels the same way and will not bless the wicked and slothful servant who fails to genuinely earn—or at least to honestly endeavor to earn—an honest day's wage.

Keep the Commandments in Faith

A final element of accepting the Lord's challenge, is to act in faith keeping all of the Lord's commandments. Both Matthew and Luke[6] record the Lord's rebuke of the scribes who paid tithing even on their herbs but omitted "judgment, mercy, and faith" from their religious practice. James E. Talmage clarifies the point, conjuring a farmer who harvests acres of wheat and then when paying tithing remembers to include a tenth of the small harvest from the herb garden. Hence, the

---

5   Joseph Fielding Smith, Gospel Doctrine, Pg. 235.
6   Matthew 23:20; Luke 11:43.

Lord's accusation of hypocrisy for paying tithes calculated to the last leaf of mint while neglecting other, weightier spiritual duties.[7] The clear implication of this message is that if we hope to have the "windows of heaven" opened on our behalf, we must attend to the weightier gospel duties.

A key theme of the Book of Mormon, repeated throughout its pages, was articulated by King Benjamin (among others), who promised the saints of his day that "if [they] would keep His commandments [they] should prosper in the land."[8] Although the first reference to tithing in the Book of Mormon was recorded 42 years after this speech, tithing was likely a part of the commandments known to those saints at that time. Even so, it was not singled out as the only or even the key requirement for the Lord's support in achieving prosperity.

The specific inclusion of "faith" on Matthew's roster of omitted practices also reminds us to exercise faith that the Lord will bless us for our obedience to the law of Tithing.

In truth, most readers will feel that they are working hard to make ends meet and that they are living the gospel—including its weightier duties—to the best of their abilities. Most will find, upon thoughtful consideration and introspection, that they simply have not made enough room to receive all the blessings that the Lord is willing to provide.

Jon M. Huntsman, Sr.

Elder Huntsman, who served for many years as an Area Seventy, was listed for years on the Forbes 400 list of the richest people in America. His company, Huntsman Corporation, is now publicly traded on the New York Stock Exchange under the ticker HUN with 2011 revenues of approximately $11 billion.

He told Forbes magazine that "At age 11 I started to pay 10% of my [income] to the Church. I was making 50 cents a day mowing lawns..." His philanthropy merely began with the Church. When he was a Naval officer, he gave $50 of his $220 per month salary to the Navy relief fund—after paying tithing. Elder Huntsman now gives $30 to $50 million to charity annually—after paying his tithing. In 1996, he gave $100 million to fund research for the cure of cancer.[9]

---

7   James E. Talmage, Jesus the Christ, Ch.31, Pg. 556 – 557.

8   Mosiah 2:22.

9   Forbes, October 13, 1997, "Deadbeat billionaires," Steve Gelsi.

But Elder Huntsman does not attribute his good fortune to merely having paid his tithing nor to his other generosity. He told the Church News that if he were to write a book about his life, "I would simply title it, 'Lucky, Lucky Me!'" He modestly credits luck and the help of others with much of his good fortune.[10]

Elder Huntsman has demonstrated that he pays his tithing, follows sound financial principles in his business and personal life, obeys the commandments and has faith in the Lord. No one who reads this text will achieve Elder Huntsman's success merely by paying tithing and following the guidelines in this book. He has been exceptionally successful. Nonetheless, by paying tithing and following his example, using the precepts outlined in this book, you can build a balance sheet to support your family and active Church service.

Practical Guide to Paying Tithes

There are some worldly considerations regarding the payment of this most sacred offering that merit brief attention.

Timing of payments: Always pay the Lord first. The best way to do this is to match your tithing checks to your paychecks. If you get paid weekly, then pay your tithes weekly. If you get paid monthly, then pay monthly. This is a clear way to demonstrate your faith in the Lord. If you can't get organized to pay with each check, then pay at least monthly.

Don't let yourself get behind. If you start trying to convince yourself that you'll "pay two months" of tithing next month, before you know it, you could easily owe more than you can imagine paying. A few hundred dollars out of each check will seem easy compared to a few thousand dollars after months of deferred payments.

A Church leader was once asked how often to pay tithing. The leader wisely responded, "as often as you want the blessings."

Gross v. Net: The Church has not stipulated whether the payment of tithes should be based on one's gross or net (after-tax) income. If your tithes and other tax deductible expenses allow you to itemize your deductions, the Federal government is subsidizing your tithing payments by up to 35%, depending on your marginal tax rate. If you are unable to itemize, the effective cost of paying 10% of your net income is roughly comparable to an itemizer's cost of paying on his gross wages. Consider the following example:

---

[10]   LDS Church News, October 25, 1997, "A true-to-life Horatio Alger saga," Gerry Avant.

Net v. Gross

Net Income Calculation	Smith	Jones
Adjusted Gross Income	$100,000	$100,000
Deductions		
Personal Exemptions	$14,800	$14,800
Standard Deduction	$11,400	
Mortgage Interest		$11,400
Deductible Tithing		$10,000
Taxable Income	$73,800	$63,800
Taxes Due		
Federal Taxes Due	$10,700	$8,720
Social Security & Medicare Taxes	$5,650	$5,650
Non-Deductible Tithing	$8,365	
After-tax, After-tithing Income	$75,285	$75,630

In this example, both the Smith and Jones families earn $100,000 per year of income. Assuming that the Smiths rent and that the Joneses own a home with a mortgage, their tax situation is different. Both families deduct their personal exemptions for the two parents and two children. The Smiths take the standard deduction and the Jones family takes the mortgage deduction, for simplicity assumed to be equal to the standard deduction. The Jones family then deducts tithing—$10,000 or 10% of the gross income. Hence, the taxable income for the two families is now different; the Smith family is taxed on $73,800 and the Jones family on $63,800. This reduces the federal tax burden of the Jones family. Both families pay the same in Social Security and Medicare taxes. Let's assume now that the Smiths pay tithing on their after tax income, meaning that they pay only $8,365 in tithing. This leaves the Smith family with after-tax, after-tithing income of $75,285. The Jones family, on the other hand, pays $1,635 more tithing and has $75,630 of after-tax, after-tithing income—$345 more than the Smiths—because they were able to deduct their tithing.

We can draw two conclusions from this example. First, based on this scenario, you can see that it was a greater sacrifice for the Smiths to pay tithing on their net income than it was for the Jones family to pay tithing on their gross income. One might therefore conclude that she need not feel guilty for paying tax on the net income (at least when there is no tax deduction for the payment of tithes).

The second conclusion one might draw from this analysis is that home ownership effectively allows you to deduct your tithing and end up with more money in your pocket after you give the Church a full 10% tithe on your gross income.

Bankruptcy: One reason to avoid bankruptcy (as if you needed another reason) is that charitable donations—such as tithing—are not always allowed. If you do pay, the Church could be required to return the money to the bankruptcy trustee.[11] If you fail to pay your tithing, even in this circumstance, you've failed to bind the Lord to his promise and you could lose your temple recommend. Consider every alternative to bankruptcy. If you must file, try to file a chapter 13 reorganization type bankruptcy, which allows for tithing payments.

Action Items:

1. Pay tithing first.
2. Pray for determination to live within your spending plan and courage to defer current spending for the sake of current investments.
3. Have faith and keep the commandments.

---

[11] Deseret News, November 8, 1997, "Debtors (spiritual) prison," Joel Campbell.

CHAPTER 5

MANAGING DEBT

My brethren, see to it that you do not put a mortgage upon the roof that covers the heads of your wives and your children. Don't do it. Don't plaster your farms with mortgages, because it is from your farms that you reap your food, and the means to provide your raiment and your other necessaries of life. Keep your possessions free from debt. Get out of debt as fast as you can, and keep out of debt, for that is the way in which the promise of God will be fulfilled to the people of his Church, that they will become the richest of all people in the world. But this will not happen while you mortgage your homes and your farms, or run into debt beyond your ability to meet your obligations; and thus, perhaps, your name and credit be dishonored because you overreached yourselves. "Never reach further than you can gather," is a good motto.

— *Joseph Fielding Smith, Gospel Doctrine, Pg.299.*

"Never Reach Further Than You Can Gather"

PRESIDENT SMITH'S ADVICE seemed rather quaint when I first read his counsel back in the 1990's. After the debt-driven economic tsunami that roiled global financial markets from 2008 through 2011, his counsel seems far more relevant and timely. Nonetheless, one would have to believe that faced with today's economics he would likely allow that some debt is necessary, particularly for the purpose of acquiring a home. On the other hand, it would be far too hasty to assume that because contemporary economics require more debt than depression era economics did that President Smith's admonition to "Never reach further than you can gather" has no relevance today.

In fact, the same general principles that guided his advice then, would guide his thoughts now. If you use your home as collateral for all your loans, you risk losing your home at the first turn of a poor economic cycle. If you charge an extravagant lifestyle on easy credit cards, a wisp of personal economic difficulty can readily make you one of the more than one million people who file bankruptcy each year.[12]

Compare the two long-term strategies suggested by the following graph, "Discretionary Spending." In this example, two dissimilar lifestyles are hypothetically compared. A Saver spends 90% of what he earns, saving 10% every year. A Spender spends 110% of what he earns, borrowing 10% every year. The cost of the interest on the accumulated debt is deducted from his discretionary spending every year. Even so, the Spender still has more discretionary income after 25 years.

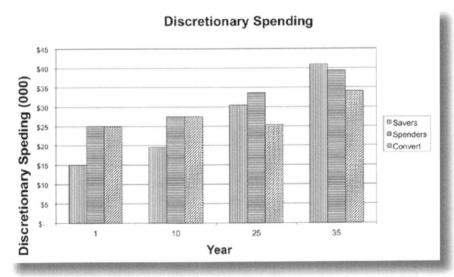

A Convert is someone, in this example, who after ten years decides to stop spending and start saving—15% per year to make up for lost time. The penalty on income during the last 25 years provides him with the least discretionary spending ability—there is a substantial penalty for not starting earlier to save.

---

12 *Deseret News*, "U.S. Consumers Filing for Bankruptcy in Record Numbers Despite Rosy Economy," August 16, 1997.

The following chart, "Debt v. Savings," compares the accumulated consumer debt or accumulated savings of a Spender to a Saver. For purposes of this example, both individuals start out with no debt and no savings. They each have the same income, $50,000 (growing 3% each year) and choose either to live beyond their means and borrow 10% of that amount each year or choose to live within their income and invest 10% of that annual amount.

After 10 years, the Saver has already accumulated $82,000 in savings (invested at 9% interest). Any income from the investment is reinvested (a wise investor allows his investments to compound by reinvesting the earnings). At the same point in time, the Spender will have a debt of $57,000 that results in an interest expense of $5,700 (at 10%) that must be deducted from his discretionary spending—most lenders won't wait to collect their interest.

After 35 years, the Saver accumulates almost $1.2 million for retirement. The Spender accumulates nothing but $300,000 of debt for his retirement. For someone with only debts accumulated later in life, there is no real retirement—about the only option to support that burden is earned income.

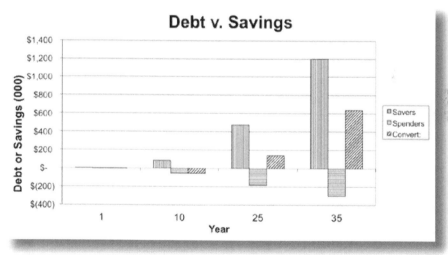

Again, the convert who starts with the same income and acts like a Spender but switches plans after ten years, accumulates debt just like the spender during the early years. Then, by investing 15% of his income—first in eliminating debt—and then in other investments, he can accumulate over $600,000 for retirement. This is certainly a good argument for converting from the spending plan to the saving plan if you find yourself on the wrong path today, but if you are just starting out you can see the tremendous benefit that comes from saving earlier. All those years of extra compounding mean that over time you'll have more discretionary income *and* more savings for retirement!

So, when you take a long-term view of spending and borrowing compared to saving and investing, the contemporary wisdom of President Smith's view of debt is established. Just because credit is easy to obtain and even seems easy to support, doesn't make it a prudent course of action. Remember President Smith's counsel, "Get out of debt as fast as you can, and keep out of debt…"

Avoiding Indentured Servitude

Credit Cards: Debt, particularly unsecured debt, binds you to your source of income. You can become virtually enslaved to your credit cards; you can become an indentured servant. No mater how much you enjoy your job, you'll enjoy it less if you know you have no option but to show up to work every day. You'll enjoy your job more and feel better about yourself, if every morning when you get up you can say confidently that you go to work because you enjoy what you do and take pride in your work product—not because your lenders insist.

Credit cards and other unsecured consumer debt are the most common contributors to bankruptcy in America. Even when exogenous events such as medical emergencies or the loss of a job trigger the disruption of cash flow, the underlying cause of the bankruptcy is carrying too much consumer debt. According to the *Wall Street Journal*, more and more the bankruptcy courts are seeing, young college educated debtors with good jobs seeking protection in bankruptcy simply because they have run up too much debt.[13]

The credit card trap is easy to fall into these days. "Have you ever paid your Visa™ bill with your MasterCard™ account?" A funny bumper sticker in the 80s became the standard way to do business in the 90s and contributed significantly to the Great Recession of the last decade when the credit card companies themselves invited you to do it, sending you pre-approved credit card applications with balance transfer options. If you make a good switch and reduce your interest rate in the process, there is some advantage. But as a more general rule, you are no better off owing the same amount of money to one lender instead of another.

One of the dangers of the balance transfer game, is how easily you can lose track of how much you owe and what it is really costing you. Have you calculated recently what your credit card interest totals each month? each

---

13   *Wall Street Journal*, "Even With a Booming Economy, Bankruptcy Filings are Surging," February 11, 1998.

year? The answer could renew your commitment to eliminate your credit card balances.

If you have some unpaid credit-card balances, the following tips can help you eliminate them.

Stop borrowing more money. Cut up the cards if you need to. Some people convince themselves that they are only taking advantage of the free loan offered by the credit card companies during the grace period. Take this quiz: if all your credit card bills came today could you pay them all off with the cash in your checking account right now? If not, you are borrowing money. The slightest interruption in your income could start you on a financial spiral that could devastate your financial plan.

Consolidate the credit card balances onto the account with the lowest interest rate. Be sure not to borrow more than 85 percent of your available credit on the card; it will make the card issuer nervous and your account could be closed.

Make more than the minimum payment. Unless you are absolutely unable to make all of your payments, paying extra on your credit card balance should be your highest financial priority. Even if the rate you are paying now is low, that teaser rate is discounted and will go up before you know it. Credit card lenders typically hope to get 15 to 18 percent interest on their accounts; they'll eventually try and get their quota from you. Pay off the debt as quickly as you can.

If you have borrowed beyond your means to repay, seek help. Contact Consumer Credit Counseling or Debt Counselors of America for help. Their services are free to you and can reduce your total monthly bill. They can negotiate permanently lower rates and lower monthly payments on your accounts while you pay them down. Using their debt repayment plan will adversely affect your credit rating, but future lenders will view this more favorably than bankruptcy.[14]

Student Loans: In contrast to credit cards, student loans seem relatively innocent. Prudent borrowing of some portion of your or your child's education may make sense in some circumstances. However, you can't sell that diploma to repay the loan. Most government sponsored student loans can never be discharged in bankruptcy. The loan will hang like an albatross around your neck even if the proceeds are invested wisely in high quality education.

Student loans should never be used to fund all of a student's education and living expenses. Even though funds are available for these purposes, education is an investment that is best funded with a large dose of

---

[14]   *Deseret News,* "Get a Handle On Credit Card Debt," Edmund Sanders, February 22, 1998.

equity. When a new business is just starting up, no one will lend it money because it is unproven. If financing is required, it usually can only be found in the form of venture capital, typically invested as equity. Even when a business matures, lenders typically make loans against tangible assets, i.e., buildings, equipment, inventory or receivables.

In personal terms, equity financing can come from several sources. The first source is money provided from savings. Grants and scholarships are also equity-type investments in education. Another form of equity financing for education is sweat equity: work-study programs, internships, and the routine jobs that occupy students on every campus and provide a critical measure of funding for education. Student loans then can fill gaps and provide the final piece of the education-financing puzzle.

Once you have student loans, you should seek to repay them as soon as you can—after repaying your credit card loans. The government sponsored student loans really have only one advantage over credit card loans—the government will generously defer payments for up to six months (a year in some cases) during documented periods of economic difficulty. (Just write to your lender and ask for a deferment if you are ever in such a circumstance.) Your credit card issuer will not likely be so patient.

One added bonus of student loans, beginning with the 1998 tax year, certain student loans are tax deductible for five years after graduating, modestly easing the cost of repayment.

Home Equity Loans: Home equity lines of credit, properly used, can provide low cost, after-tax credit. These loans are most appropriately used to fund home improvements. (Though it is better still to fund home improvements from savings.) They can also be used to repay credit card balances. This step should only be taken in rare instances when the alternative of repaying the credit card loan directly from earnings over a short number of years is not a viable option.

You never want to borrow money on your home equity loan to pay for disposable purchases, such as, vacations or extravagant toys, like boats and all-terrain vehicles. Using a home equity loan for shorter-lived asset purchases such as computers or even cars is a bad idea. You could use up the asset before you ever get around to paying off the debt and you'll be in no position to purchase a replacement.

Borrowing against your home's equity is risky. If the value of your home drops, the home equity loan can quickly turn your castle into a cage. If you should have an interruption of income at the same time that property values are down—these two events are often correlated as we've seen in the last few years—you may lose your home or could even be forced to file bankruptcy.

Mortgage Loans: Mortgage loans are typically our largest debts and so provide the greatest opportunity for saving money over the long term. If you can reduce the interest rate on your loan by refinancing, you can save thousands of dollars. When you do refinance, be sure to focus on the permanent change in the interest rate; don't focus on the payment. If you've been paying on your mortgage and refinance with a new thirty-year loan, your payment will go down even if the rate doesn't drop much because you are extending the term of the loan. On the other hand, if you reduce the rate substantially, but shorten the term of the loan to 20 or even 15 years from 30 years, you may even pay more on a monthly basis, but you'll be making a larger principal payment every month. That increase in principal is virtually money in the bank.

Auto Loans: Auto loans can be refinanced, too. Typically there are no fees, so if rates in the market drop or your credit rating improves; if you have an opportunity to refinance your loan at a lower rate, take it. But don't fall to the temptation to extend the term of the loan. A drop in interest rate won't affect the car payment like it will on the mortgage payment because a bigger portion of your car payment already goes to principal, but even a few dollars a month will help. Try to reduce the term of the loan if you can. In this way, you'll eliminate a debt sooner than you would otherwise.

Once the car loan is paid off, don't rush right out to buy a new car. Keep making the payments—to yourself. Wait to buy a new car until you can buy it with the cash you've saved and the value of the car you'll trade in.

The Dangers of Debt Consolidation and Refinancing

The lure of debt consolidation or mortgage refinancing is typically the lower payment(s) that result from the process. Consumers can be easily confused by the complex disclosure documents and confusing terms associated with most debt consolidation loans. Amidst this confusion, consumers can wind up paying significant fees, higher interest rates or higher total interest payments, and, if habits don't change, still more debt.

The typical fee structure for a first mortgage loan involves a 1% origination fee, additional "points," each one equal to one percent of the mortgage, and a slew of other miscellaneous fees that can total over one percent of the loan amount again. For a typical, high quality (high credit score) mortgage refinance, total fees can easily top two to three percent of the mortgage amount. For a $200,000 mortgage, fees could add up to $6,000 to the loan balance—even if you shop well and get a fair deal. It could take years of lower interest rates to make up for the cost of these fees. You can sometimes find lenders willing to refinance larger mortgages for no fee—so long as you are willing to accept a rate somewhat above market. If you are considering a move or think interest rates may drop further, such a plan makes sense. In most cases, however, you are better off with the lower rate.

In the event that you are forced to seek a debt consolidation loan from a sub-prime lender, you can expect to pay 10% of the loan amount—or more—up front. The lender may loan you the money to pay the up front fees, but that doesn't mean you're not paying it. If you sign a promissory note for $20,000 but receive only $18,000, you'll have to repay all $20,000. If after just two years you are able to refinance the debt with a bank or credit union with no fees at a lower rate, consider that the 10% origination fee will have added 5% per year to the cost of borrowing the money.

Another risk of refinancing or consolidating debts is that you may end up paying a higher interest rate. If you focus on reducing your monthly payment, you may find that you are refinancing some debts with lower rates with a new loan at a higher rate. Keep in mind, that typical car loans have lower rates than debt consolidation loans.

Even if you are genuinely obtaining a lower rate of interest on your refinance, many debt consolidation vehicles, home equity lines particularly, provide low payment options. This may tempt you to not to pay off the obligation as quickly as you would have repaid the debt had you kept it on your credit card, car loan or student loan. If you keep the debt longer, even if you lower the interest rate, over time you'll likely pay more interest.

A final risk of debt consolidation and refinancing, is that reduced payments may make it easier for you to borrow more money. The old, higher payments were more difficult to make, but they may have provided you with discipline that the new easy payments don't. As you refinance or consolidate debts, remember that if you run up more bills, you may not have the ability to refinance or consolidate again.

If you do refinance your mortgage or consolidate debts, be sure to cut up your credit cards and close the accounts that you consolidate so that you can't run up the balances again. Even if you reduce your scheduled payments, pay more than the minimum every month. Virtually all loans are written today without prepayment penalties—make the largest payment you can afford.

There are some reasons that do justify debt consolidation. If your income drops or you are hoping to reduce your household income, i.e., so one parent can stay home with young children, it makes sense to consolidate your debts to achieve the lowest possible monthly payment to allow for the new lower income level.

Another time to consider a debt consolidation loan is in preparation for the purchase of a home. Well before you actually make an offer on a home, or apply for a mortgage, you'll want to consolidate debts and begin setting aside your excess cash for a down payment. Be cautious not to overreach when you buy the home; the additional debt you are carrying may make it difficult to keep up on the payments.

Finally, if you have overextended yourself, lured by offers of easy and seemingly inexpensive credit, and if you have learned your lesson and are prepared to cut up the credit cards, then a debt consolidation loan of some type may make sense. In this situation, however, if you are forced to borrow money at unusually high rates of interest, you should give serious consideration, instead, to seeking help from a not-for-profit consumer credit management service.

Investment Leverage

Barron's defines investment leverage as a "means of enhancing return or value without increasing investment.[15]" Buying investment property, a duplex, for instance, with some of your own money and some money borrowed from the bank is a familiar example of investment leverage. Leverage increases both the risk and the potential return on an investment.

Because of the prospect for higher returns, we are often tempted to make genuine investments in a highly leveraged fashion—with loads of borrowed money. Worse, we sometimes try to define consumer spending as wise investment leverage.

When you buy a car with a loan, that isn't leverage. The car will depreciate—quickly. There is no return on investment for a car, therefore, you can't increase the return on your equity or down payment by borrowing part of the purchase price.

Even though your home will likely appreciate, providing a modest return, it is still not appropriate to think of a home as an investment or the mortgage as leverage. You own a home primarily as a utilitarian device to protect you and your family from the elements. The risk of loss of value is very real; the loss of value is often associated with a poor job market, creating the possibility that the loss of value of your home could be associated with the loss of your income. With your home in foreclosure, you would hardly want to explain to your family that as a highly sophisticated investor, you had highly levered your home purchase to increase the potential return.

---

[15]   *Dictionary of Finance and Investment Terms,* Barron's Educational Series, Inc., 1991.

Another temptation is to allow credit card balances to grow in the name of making investments for retirement. Perhaps your employer will match a 401(K) investment, you really shouldn't pass up on the opportunity to get the match. But borrowing on credit cards to do it is dangerous and is not a genuine case of investment leverage. If you need to pay off the credit cards at some point in the future, the 401(K) monies are not readily available. Even if you can qualify for a hardship disbursement, the funds are subject to taxes and penalties that can eat up half the money—there goes the employer match. There goes your investment return. There goes your leverage. While it is vital that you contribute to your 401(K) or other retirement plan, you need to make that investment without running up additional debt.

A final example of poor justification for borrowing under the guise of leverage is borrowing on credit cards or even on a home equity loan to pay for home improvements. Of course you can add such costs to the cost basis of your home for tax purposes. Home improvements, however, rarely increase the value of the home as much as they cost. Even if the improvements add substantially to the value of the home when they are new, they will begin to depreciate with use. The brand new kitchen, for example, will only be considered "new" for a short time. Once the new kitchen shows signs of use, the increase in value of your home due to the new kitchen may be rather small. Home improvements are best made from savings rather than new debt. You always want to leave as much room as possible between the value of your home and the sum of the mortgages pledged against it.

Once you have established an appropriately large, conservative investment fund for your retirement, children's education and missions, you may have the ability to begin to invest a small portion of your savings in leveraged investments.

Rental property may be a good investment if you have experience with real estate or have substantial skills in the home maintenance area. Most banks like to see a 30% down payment for investment property. During the middle part of the last decade, many lenders allowed all sorts of crazy things in real estate lending, ultimately creating a global recession that continues to haunt millions of Americans who lost their homes as a result. While you may be able to find someone still willing to lend you more than 70% of a real estate investment purchase, you should really avoid over-levering your investment. Consider the following two hypothetical examples that demonstrate the risk of leverage:

Scenario A	2012	2015
Property Value		
Value	$ 200,000	$ 160,000
Loan Balance	$ 140,000	$ 136,536
Equity	$ 60,000	$ 23,464
Monthly Operation		
Monthly Rent	$ 2,000	$ 1,800
Mortgage Payment	$ 1,076	$ 1,076
Other Expenses	$ 500	$ 500
Net Monthly Profit/(Loss)	$ 424	$ 224

Scenario B	2012	2015
Property Value		
Value	$ 200,000	$ 160,000
Loan Balance	$ 180,000	$ 175,546
Equity	$ 20,000	-$ 15,546
Monthly Operation		
Monthly Rent	$ 2,000	$ 1,800
Mortgage Payment	$ 1,384	$ 1,384
Other Expenses	$ 500	$ 500
Net Monthly Profit/(Loss)	$ 116	-$ 84

In both cases, the investors purchase a duplex costing $200,000. In scenario A, the investor makes a customary 30% down payment and the property starts out generating $2,000 per month rent. At this rate, the investor profits $424 per month after making the mortgage payment (calculated using 8.5% for 30 years) and covering other expenses including taxes, insurance and maintenance. In scenario B, the investor makes only a 10% down payment. His identical property only nets $116 per month because the mortgage payment is higher.

In both scenarios, the value of the property drops 20% over three years (much less than the declines we saw from 2007 to 2010 in many places in America) and the rental rate also drops 10%. Investor A is unhappy because he has lost $40,000 of value, but he still has a safe equity cushion of almost $24,000 and a positive cash flow of $224 per month. Investor B, however, has lost his entire investment and is suffering a monthly loss of $84 per month. The property can't be sold to pay off the loan (which was most likely personally guaranteed) and the property no longer generates enough cash flow to service the debt. Not much of an investment.

The same risks apply to levering investments in stocks, bonds and mutual funds. If you have capital that you can afford to lose without risking your retirement plans, children's education or missions, you may consider prudent amounts of leverage. If you do leverage stocks, be sure to lever a portfolio of various stocks rather than the purchase of a single stock. The risk of a portfolio of a dozen stocks (or more) dramatically declining in value is far lower than the risk for any individual stock. If the value of the investments in a brokerage account falls, the broker will call you and ask you to put more cash into the account to reduce the debt or the broker will sell your stocks to pay off the debt. In order to avoid or at least reduce this risk, you may wish to borrow even less than the broker allows against the assets in your account.

Finally, don't ever borrow money against your house to invest in the stock market. You wouldn't want to lose your house and your savings in the same day.

Action Items:

1. Pay off your debts as quickly as possible, following this hierarchy:
   a. Credit cards and other unsecured consumer debt.
   b. Student loans.
   c. Home equity loans and other secured consumer debt (except car loans).
   d. Car loans
   e. Mortgage loans.
2. Be cautious when refinancing.
3. Don't use credit cards or home equity to lever your investments—be patient and save.

CHAPTER 6
OWNING A CAR (or small fleet)

The wise man is, therefore, going to steer his course away from the living death of pleasure-seeking. He is not going into bondage or debt to buy automobiles and other costly equipages to keep pace with the rush of fashionable pleasure-seeking, in this respect. He is not going to borrow money to satisfy the popular craze for traveling in Europe or in our own country, with no purpose in view but pleasure. He is not going to grow nervous and gray in a struggle for means that his wife and daughter, for mere pleasure, may spend the summer at costly, fashionable resorts, or in distant lands. It is true that there are many in our community who do not appear to be wise, and who are doing just these and other foolish acts for so called pleasure.

— Joseph Fielding Smith, Gospel Doctrine, Pg.323

Why a Chapter on Cars?

A CHAPTER ON CARS in a book on financial planning may seem out of place, but when you consider that the average five year cost of owning even an economical new car like a Ford Fiesta exceeds $24,000 you begin to appreciate the value of this chapter.[16] Over your

---

[16]   Intellichoice, www.intellichoice.com, January 6, 2012.

lifetime, you will likely spend more to buy, maintain, insure, fuel and finance your cars than you will pay for your home.

We get so accustomed to the financial burden of our automobiles that we sometimes forget what they really cost us. If you have two, three or even four vehicles as some large families do, the cost of owning the vehicles can easily exceed the cost of owning your home. Over time, your home (or at least the land it sits on) may appreciate. If you drive your car, no matter how nice it is and no matter how well you care for it, it depreciates. It also needs fuel or electricity, insurance, maintenance, and interest expense on financing (even if you paid cash, the car has tied up capital and that has a cost).

The purpose of this chapter is to discuss ways to reduce the cost of car ownership over the long run. Whether you like to buy a new car every two years, or are driving the VW Beetle your parents bought for your high school graduation when bell bottoms were in style, the principles discussed in this chapter can be applied to your benefit.

Buying a Car

It costs a lot of money to buy a car. Most of us tend to think of the cost of a car as something of a capital investment. The car is tangible, solid and provides the valuable function of moving us from place to place. A surprising amount of the car's initial purchase cost, however, is permanently lost.

Sales Tax: When you buy a car in most states, a sales tax payment of up to 8% of the purchase price is required. With the average price of a new car now in excess of $20,000, that amount can range from $1,000 to $2,000 or more. Sales tax is not an asset. You cannot sell it to the next car purchaser. The money is gone. Forever.

Profit and Overhead: In most cases, when you purchase a car—new or used, it will be from a dealer or from someone who does this for a living. They have resources to back up their sale of the car with a warranty or "certification" of fitness. If you drive the car off the lot and try to sell it, you'll not be able to make the same warranties and cannot afford to do as much advertising and can't spend as much time in an effort to sell it. As a result, there is a margin of profit and overhead that you can't recover when you sell a car.

Fees: All cars must be registered and tagged—for a fee. New cars also come with an assortment of bonus fees, chief among them the destination charge. These fees add nothing to the value of the car and you typically can't sell them when you sell the car. Hence, these fees are lost as well.

Depreciation: A car depreciates quickly. After accounting for dealer profit and sales taxes, your car depreciates about 10% per year—some more, some less—but about 10% each year. This means, that after allowing for sales tax, dealer profit and the first year of depreciation, you may lose 15-25% of what you paid for the car in just the first year. Buying a used car helps, but remember that you still pay sales tax at the same rate, you still pass along some dealer profit—or take some additional risk buying the car in a private sale. Even a used car continues to depreciate and requires maintenance.

Conclusion: Don't buy a car.

Really. Keep the one you have as long as you can stand it. Use mass transit as much as you can conveniently do it. If you can eliminate a car from your fleet, even the cheapest car, you can easily save over $4,000 per year.

If you must, tips for buying a car

There are three keys to making a successful car purchase: 1) choose wisely, 2) negotiate well, and 3) when buying a used car, check it thoroughly.

Choose wisely: There is a vast amount of data available now to help you make an informed decision about a car. In addition to all that is written in the auto magazines about new cars, *Consumer Reports* publishes an annual car issue that outsells any of their other monthly reports.

Money magazine also publishes an annual auto report that keys on value by comparing the purchase price of the car to the five-year cost of ownership provided by Intellichoice. This information is also helpful, particularly when choosing among similar vehicles. Keep in mind, however, that even though the ratio of ownership costs to purchase price may be lower for a Porsche than a Ford, the Ford is still cheaper to own.

Negotiate well: When you purchase a car there are several tips to remember to reduce the dent in your retirement planning.

Don't go to the dealership until you have narrowed your purchase decision to a few, select models. For each model you are considering, you should know the dealer's invoice, rebates, and, when possible, whether there are currently any factory-to-dealer incentives offered on the car (this information is widely available on-line). While such incentives are not passed along directly to you, these incentives may make it possible for you to negotiate a deal at *less than* the dealer invoice. Even without such incentives, you should be able to negotiate a price just 3% to 7% above dealer invoice.[17]

---

[17]   *Money,* "6th Annual Car Buyer's Guide," March 1, 1997, pp 142.

Next, avoid the back office bump. After going 15 rounds to negotiate your best deal with the sales department, most dealerships force you to go a bonus round with the office manager. The location and configuration of the office is intentionally intimidating, to make you feel as though you are trapped. The office manager will offer you an extended warranty, rust proofing, seat protectors, credit life insurance, and trim packages. None of these options is likely to be fairly priced. This is the dealer's last hope to make up the profit you negotiated away out front.

Check out used cars carefully: As with new cars, *Consumer Reports*, *Money*, and other publications review used cars. The Intellichoice web page offers tremendous volumes of current information on used cars as well. This information includes valuation information. When selecting a used car, you may wish to follow this three-step plan:

Research: First select a few models to choose from by reading up on the cars you are interested in. Evaluate the costs of ownership, including insurance, maintenance and depreciation. You can easily determine the market value of the cars that interest you by checking on-line with Kelly Bluebook or Intellichoice. The local classifieds will also provide a good indication of value in your local market (but remember, asking prices will be higher than the sales prices for private sales).

Inspect the Car: Don't just give the car a quick test drive, use a checklist. Also, check the car's title. CarFax allows you to enter the Vehicle Identification Number and receive a report showing the car's history, including major accidents. Checking the title is particularly important when you purchase a car from an individual whom you don't know. Unscrupulous, unlicensed dealers—called curbstoners—may try to sell you high-priced junk (or worse) and then disappear.[18]

Mechanic Inspection: You probably don't want to pay your mechanic to check out every car you consider, that's why you do a preliminary inspection. But once you've found a car that meets your requirements, you may want to have a pro give it a final inspection to be sure that there are no surprises. If you buy a car merely because it is for sale below your educated estimate of market value, beware that you could lose your entire pricing advantage if a major repair is required as soon as you drive the car home.

Financing A Car

Nothing is likely to influence your car purchase more than the monthly payment you can afford right now. Caught between budgets and desires

---

[18]   *Good Housekeeping*, "Best Buys in Nearly New Cars," September 1, 1997, p 158.

to drive nicer, newer, safer, more reliable or bigger cars, some consumers are falling into the trap offered by tantalizing, low lease payments. The dealer probably didn't tell you that leasing was a trap. In contrast, if you develop a long-term strategy you can avoid having a car loan ever again within just four years.

The Leasing Trap: Most leases are pitched by drawing attention to low payments over a relatively short period of time, say two to four years. There are a number of complex variables that can be used to artificially lower the lease payment such that the total life of lease cost is actually higher than you expect. For instance, a down payment or even a deposit accelerates the cash flow to the lessor. Excessive mileage fees, disposition fees, excessive wear and tear charges, and high purchase options can be used to lock you into paying more than you realized.[19]

Even if you understand your lease terms completely and are satisfied with the explicit risks, you may not be considering the single largest risk. By leasing the vehicle, you ensure that you will always have a car payment if you have a car. In a typical lease, you are paying a relatively high portion of the car's purchase price over the lease term to use up a small portion of the vehicle's useful life.

Dealers and lessors will tell you that leasing cars makes sense for people who like to buy a new car every few years. While that is true, it makes little financial sense to buy a new car every few years.

Long-term Strategy: It will take some time, but if you plan carefully, you can pay cash for your cars and follow the age old adage of the wise man—earn interest, don't pay it. The strategy is simple, first purchase a car that you can afford to finance over no more than four years. Then keep it for three years past the last payment you make on the loan. This strategy will allow you to purchase this car's replacement without any financing—even allowing for inflation. The key is to keep making the payment after the loan is paid off, depositing the monthly payments into your savings account—a separate one intended just for the new car.

Look up the payment you can afford in the left hand column of the accompanying table. Then, moving right across the columns, find the first acceptable loan balance—don't settle too quickly for the five year term—it makes the strategy much more difficult to accomplish because you'll have to keep the car for so long. If you have a large family and need to purchase a large vehicle, such as a Suburban, merely to provide seats and seatbelts for the whole family to travel together at one time, you may need to follow a longer-term plan.

---

19   *Deseret News,* "The Car Question," April 21, 1997.

Car Financing Affordability

PMT	Term (in Years)			
	2 Years	3 Years	4 Years	5 Years
$ 150	$3,300	$4,752	$6,086	$7,311
$ 200	$4,400	$6,336	$8,114	$9,748
$ 250	$5,500	$7,920	$10,143	$12,185
$ 300	$6,600	$9,503	$12,171	$14,622
$ 350	$7,700	$11,087	$14,200	$17,059
$ 400	$8,800	$12,671	$16,228	$19,496
$ 450	$9,900	$14,255	$18,257	$21,934
$ 500	$11,000	$15,839	$20,285	$24,371
$ 550	$12,100	$17,423	$22,314	$26,808
$ 600	$13,200	$19,007	$24,342	$29,245

Example: If you can afford a $350 per month payment, you can afford to borrow $14,200 at 8.5% interest toward your next car.

When you purchase the car, put as much cash down as you can afford. Even if you don't have any cash but must buy a car, don't let yourself get trapped into a lease. Most credit unions will finance 100% of a car purchase for customers with good credit. Stick with the long-term strategy.

The first thing you'll discover with this strategy is that you can buy much less vehicle than you could with a lease. If you lease a car at the same payment as you could purchase one on a four-year loan basis, you could probably lease twice as much car. Consider, however, that after seven years, if you lease you will be on your third or fourth brand new car and you'll have a lease payment that is easily 20% higher than the one you started with. If you buy, pay off your car in four years and keep making the payment into a savings account for three more years, you could have a brand new car in the garage with no car payment at all.

Now, your patience and commitment can really begin to pay off. If you continue to make the original car payment into a savings account every month, you can move up scale on every subsequent car purchase—just be sure not to replace the car too often. Remember, the years of highest depreciation are the early years. If you replace the car every seven years or so, you can move upscale each time.

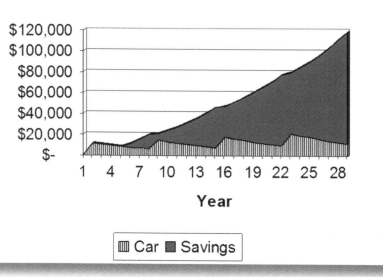

Value of Car Plus Savings

Year

Car ■ Savings

Or, if you are genuinely committed to building and planning for the future, replace the car every seven years with a newer model of the same car or a similar car—don't move further upscale. In this way, the initial car payment will create an investment fund that can easily pay for missionary service during retirement. After 28 years of executing the strategy with a $350 monthly payment earning interest at just five percent annually, you would have a brand new car (your fifth) and $85,000 in the bank. If you had been leasing, yes you could still be driving a nicer new car but you'd have a lease payment that over the years would have grown from $350 to around $800 per month and you'd have nothing in savings.

If you still want to lease, you must really love the smell of a new car.

Maintaining a Car

If you are going to keep a car for seven years at a time, you'll need to be thinking more about maintenance than you have if you've been leasing or turning your car over more regularly.

If you plan to keep your car for seven years, it is vitally important that you give the car proper maintenance from the very start. Follow the manufacturer's recommendations to the letter. You may even want to change the oil more often than recommended.

One of the easiest ways to reduce car maintenance and repair expenses is to do some of them yourself. Most of the cost of a repair is typically labor. If you can do it yourself, that cost is saved.

You may be tempted to argue that your time is too valuable because at your day job you make, say, $20 per hour and it would take you two or three times longer than the mechanic to do the job making it cheaper to have the mechanic do it.

This could be true if you were taking time off of work and getting docked for the time—if you work on salary the point is moot. And almost everyone gets some time off. If, in those free hours, you engage in activities that save you money, it is just as good as making money. Remember, the tax effect of saving money can double the value of the money saved compared to earning additional wages. If the mechanic charges $40 (the minimum) for a task that takes him 15 minutes and takes you 45 minutes (three times as long), you are better off even if you believe that your time is worth $20 per hour. In this example, you save $40 in 45 minutes. In comparison, it would take you two hours to earn $40 gross wages. But it would take you three to four hours (depending on your marginal tax rate) to increase your paycheck enough to actually bring home $40 extra after tax. It may be easier than you think to "earn" $40 per hour as a mechanic.

Almost no one who isn't a professional mechanic can do all of the maintenance or much of the repairs required on newer cars. That said, there are some routine maintenance items almost anyone can learn to do with a little help from a *Chilton's* car maintenance and repair manual.

The bottom line here is not that you should do all of the maintenance and repairs on your car—or even all that you could figure out how to do. If you just do *more* on your own than you have, you should be better off.

Another key to keeping your car healthy for the seven-year plan is treating the car right when you drive it. Quick starts and stops put unnecessary wear and tear on the engine, transmission and brakes. Racing full speed over bumps, potholes and railroad tracks not only stresses the suspension but also loosens nuts, bolts and welds all over the car. Each bump imperceptibly does its part. If you drive cautiously and carefully on bad roads and observe warnings about bumps and tracks you preserve your car's condition.[20]

One final note about car care. Keep your car clean. This will not only preserve the car's finish and interior surfaces, but it will also help you to take pride of ownership that should translate into better care in other areas. If you don't feel ashamed to be driving this car, you're likely to drive more carefully and to perform the scheduled maintenance in a timely way.

---

[20] Tom and Ray Magliozzi and Doug Berman, *Ten Ways You May Be Ruining Your Car Without Even Knowing It!* King Features Syndicate, 1993.

Selling Your Old Car

If you follow the seven-year plan, you won't often have to worry about how to dispose of your car, but when you do there are a few considerations to bear in mind.

The first thing to do when you sell your car is to find out how much it is worth. There are three sources—and you may want to check them all—that are good indicators of value.

Classified advertising in your local paper is generally sorted by year, make and model thereby making comparisons relatively easy.

The Kelly Bluebook values available on the Internet provide a clear indication of value range, indicating retail and trade-in values. You should expect your final selling price to be closer to the trade-in value.

Finally, Intellichoice provides value estimates on its web page.

Remember that as an individual, you'll not be able to achieve as high a price as a reputable dealer. These dealers typically conduct a thorough inspection and make repairs to put the car in top shape. Then, they may provide 30 day guarantees or even return policies. You can't compete with their service, convenience, ad budget and reputation. Don't expect to get as much for your car.

Trade-In: It is unquestionably easier to trade your car in as partial payment for the newer one you are purchasing—its also the best way to get the least value for your car. In virtually all cases, the dealer will be willing take it off your hands. Beware that the dealer may be using the trade-in as a way to mask the amount you are really paying for the car. Before you begin the negotiations, make sure you know the value of both the car you are buying and the car you are trading.

In most states, there is also a significant sales tax benefit to trading your car in. The amount of the trade in is deducted from the total purchase price when calculating the sales tax due on your new car. On a $5,000 trade-in, the savings could be several hundred dollars.

Private Sale: If you think buying a car is difficult, you haven't tried selling one. Unless you have priced the car painfully low, you'll likely spend weeks running advertisements that can be expensive. You may be tempted to park the car in a row of other cars for sale along some major thoroughfare, but beware, it is dangerous and it may be illegal. You may be ticketed—or even towed—for parking your car in some places for more than 24 hours. Furthermore, you may find that the stereo disappears well before the rest of the car. The cost of a window and stereo could total more than the difference between the private sale value and the trade-in value. Just the cost of advertisements, and the capital cost of holding the car for what could turn out to be weeks or even months, can eat up any private sale premium you hope to keep.

The value of conducting a private sale is probably greater for a more valuable car. But, if you are executing the seven-year strategy, the old car won't be worth much relative to the new car. It may be easier to just trade it in.

Implications for Latter-day Saints

Most people think of their cars as symbols of their personal values. If you execute the strategy recommended in this chapter, you may be driving smaller, older, cheaper cars than you would if you had ignored this chapter. So, whenever you see your clean, well maintained, smaller-older-cheaper car, remind yourself that this car says you are thrifty and smart.

Remember, too, that driving a smaller car is part of your strategy to serve in the Church. Over the years, the money this strategy saves will go a long way toward paying for your children's missions and education. It can even contribute to your own mission fund in retirement.

Action Items:

1. Own as few cars as is practical for your family.
2. Drive each car for as long as is practical for your situation.
3. After a car is paid for, make the monthly payment to your savings account and pay cash for the next car.
4. Take good care of your car and do some of the maintenance yourself.

CHAPTER 7

OWNING A HOME

What was taught in the early days of our history in this intermountain region is equally true today, and it is the duty of every Latter-day Saint, so far as it is possible, to own his home, to possess an earthly inheritance.

— *Joseph Fielding Smith, Gospel Doctrine, Pg.306*

Why Own a Home?

A HOME OF YOUR own can provide key, long-term stability for your family. Because it is so much more difficult to buy and sell a home than to rent an apartment, a home purchase tends to cause us to put down roots, develop friendships and other relationships in our neighborhood and ward. Over the long term, a home also provides financial stability.

Often times, people think of a home as an investment. Over the long-term a home—or at least the lot it sits on—will appreciate. But over the years, it also requires substantial maintenance and repair, offsetting much of the slow appreciation. As the last few years have shown, as an investment, homes have proven to be risky.

Financially, the value of the home to your family may be that the mortgage payment won't rise over the years (presuming it's a fixed rate loan). Renters generally find that their rent increases year after year, making it difficult to escape the rental treadmill.

Another benefit of homeownership depends on your commitment to pay off the mortgage prior to retirement. If you do pay off the mortgage, you'll have a virtually free place to live after you retire, reducing your need for income during those years and making the possibility to serve a mission considerably greater.

Buying a Home

The key to buying a home is preparation. If you are following the principles in this book, you should be ready to own a home in a relatively short time. You should already have savings for a down payment and little debt to impair your ability to borrow money for a home. To make your goal of homeownership a reality, simply follow these last few steps.

Prepare yourself financially. During the final few months prior to purchasing a home, there are some important guidelines to follow, in addition to those discussed elsewhere in this book. The overriding rule during these months is to simplify. Specifically, avoid changing jobs, borrowing money, major purchases or even paying off debts early. Defer purchases until after you are in your new home and you are sure you can afford them. Borrowing money—or even trying—can add a wrinkle to your loan application that it is best to avoid. If you have extra cash to pay off debt, your loan officer can arrange for you to do so at closing—large money movements prior to closing can confuse underwriters and cause needless frustration for you in trying to document all of your cash flows.[21]

Anticipate closing costs: With lenders offering home loans with very small down payments, closing costs can represent up to 50% or more of the cash you may be required to pay at closing. One technique that may work, particularly in a soft real estate market, is to negotiate to have the seller pay part or all of your closing costs. The following is a short list of closing costs for the purchase of a $150,000 home with a 5% down payment.

Fee Description	Fee Amount
Loan Origination Fee (1% of loan)	$1,425.00
Lender's Title Insurance	$500.00
Appraisal	$350.00
Credit Report	$50.00
Processing Fee	$200.00
Underwriting Fee	$300.00
Settlement Fee	$100.00
Tax Service Fee	$100.00
Total	$3,025.00

---

[21]   *Deseret News*, "Planning can ease pain of shopping for house," September 14, 1997.

In addition, you will likely have to pay some prepaid interest that could total almost a full mortgage payment depending upon when in the month you close. You will also have to purchase a homeowners insurance policy and pay a portion of the property taxes that will come due within the year. These amounts can also be material and are not usually considered closing costs, *per se*, in the mortgage industry.

Choose a real estate agent. For most people, it is imperative to find a good real estate agent. Traditionally, real estate agents have worked for real estate sellers—even the agents who seem to represent buyers. Because the seller pays the commission, agents have had to look out for the seller. More recently, buyer's agents and brokers have become more common. Find a good one on a reference from a friend who was treated fairly by the agent and then enter into a written agreement setting out her responsibilities as your agent. Typically, she will still get her commission from the seller, but she'll put the seller's agent on notice that she works for you.[22]

Find a loan officer and get pre-qualified. It is important, when you are early in the process of looking for a home, to have a loan officer help you test your ability to qualify for a loan, given your down payment savings, your household income and other debts. Your real estate agent may recommend a loan officer. You may also be able to get a good recommendation from a friend. Be cautious about whom you deal with; rates and fees and the ability to get loans closed successfully vary significantly from one loan officer to another. A good loan officer can quickly help you determine what size loan you may qualify to borrow. This will give you a good idea about your price range.[23]

The following table provides a sample range of monthly income and mortgage affordability at various interest rates—presuming you have few other debts and good credit.

Monthly Income	Interest Rate		
	3%	4%	5%
$2,000	$118,595	$104,731	$93,141
$2,500	$148,243	$130,913	$116,426
$3,000	$177,892	$157,096	$139,711
$3,500	$207,541	$183,279	$162,996
$4,000	$237,189	$209,461	$186,282
$4,500	$266,838	$235,644	$209,567
$5,000	$296,487	$261,827	$232,852

[22] Money Insider, "Buying a home? You May Want a Broker on Your side," January 11, 1998.
[23] Deseret News, "Planning can ease pain of shopping for house," September 14, 1997.

Monthly Income	Interest Rate		
	3%	4%	5%
$5,500	$326,135	$288,009	$256,137
$6,000	$355,784	$314,192	$279,422
$6,500	$385,433	$340,375	$302,708
$7,000	$415,081	$366,557	$325,993
$7,500	$444,730	$392,740	$349,278
$8,000	$474,379	$418,922	$372,563
$8,500	$504,027	$445,105	$395,848
$9,000	$533,676	$471,288	$419,134
$9,500	$563,325	$497,470	$442,419
$10,000	$592,973	$523,653	$465,704

Today's historically low interest rates combined with depressed real estate prices in many markets make 2012 a good year to make a prudent home purchase, despite the risks.

The data in the table presumes the use of a 30-year fixed mortgage. Your actual ability to qualify for a loan will be determined by a number of factors, including property taxes and hazard insurance—factors that are difficult to estimate across geographic regions. Be sure to consult with your loan officer.

Work as a team. From this point forward, work as a team to find a house, finance the purchase and celebrate your new home. By working as a team, your loan officer can tell you quickly whether the homes you are seeing are in your price range. Furthermore, your real estate agent will quickly develop an understanding of your tastes and objectives. Finally, when you've found a home, your loan file should be largely complete, allowing the closing to be scheduled quickly—which may be a big advantage if you are bidding against someone else.

Home inspection: There really should be two thorough home inspections done before you close on your home—plus an appraisal. All of these steps may be required by the lender to protect its interest in your home, but these steps also protect you. You should complete the first inspection yourself. It will help you evaluate the candidate properties more objectively. After you've written an offer, you will want to hire an inspector to more thoroughly inspect the home, its systems and structure to be sure that no unnoticed defects are present. The lender may require that an inspection be done. If not, they'll want a copy of the one you commission.

Your real estate agent may advise you to write your purchase offer with a "contingency" for a satisfactory inspection, giving you an automatic out if something unsatisfactory turns up in the final inspection.

Financing a Home

Nothing in the process of buying a home is likely to be as traumatic, challenging, and potentially humiliating as applying for a loan. Even the most successful professionals, attorneys, doctors, accountants can feel intimidated by having their most important purchase tied up in the proverbial "loan committee." Here are a few key tips for making the process easier.

At the outset, you need to know what to expect. The underwriter will want to know everything about your finances. Everything. This is particularly true for first time home buyers with small down payments. For instance, in order to be approved for a loan, you will need to not only document that you have cash for the down payment, but you'll need to document the source. The underwriter may be concerned that you have borrowed the down payment and hence, may have additional debt service and a lower commitment to the home because little or none of your own money is invested.

The following table outlines some of the things the underwriter will wish to establish, the reason the lender wants to know, and the means generally used to verify the required information.

Objective	Purpose	Method of Verification
Adequate funds for down payment and closing costs.	Establish that the purchaser/borrower has a substantial commitment to taking care of the home and making the loan payments.	Bank statements and / or direct verification with bank of current and average balance. Funds should be readily accessible.
Cash reserves of 2 months of total debt obligations.	Establish that in the event of an interruption in cash flow, funds will be available to make the mortgage payment.	Bank statements and / or direct verification with bank of current and average balance. Funds may be in a retirement account.

Objective	Purpose	Method of Verification
Mortgage payment (after closing) of less than 28% of monthly income.	Establish that there will be adequate funds to cover the mortgage payment each month.	Loan payment will be calculated by lender; includes property taxes, homeowners insurance, and private mortgage insurance (if required).
Total monthly obligations less than 36% of monthly income.	Establish that there will be adequate funds to cover the mortgage payment each month— even with all of your other debts.	Total monthly obligations must be established on the credit report. Occasionally, errors are found; your loan officer should work with you to resolve them.
Demonstrate a pattern of paying bills in a timely way.	The lender wants not only to be paid, but also to be paid on time each month; the lender will look to your payment history with other creditors for reassurance.	The lender will review your credit report for this information. You may work with your loan officer to correct mistakes or explain extenuating circumstances.
Evidence of a stable employment history and income.	The lender wants to be sure that not only are you currently earning an adequate income, but that you have done so consistently.	The lender will seek employment verifications from each of your past employers for the most recent two years. W-2 forms and pay-stubs may suffice.

It will typically take two to three weeks to prepare a loan file for underwriting. The appraisal and title report are almost completely out of your control; be sure to allow plenty of time for this process to be completed in the purchase contract. Homebuyers sometimes balk at the process, refusing to provide this or that item. Inevitably, this slows the process and ultimately the underwriter gets what she wants. Once the file is complete, underwriting may take several days to more than a week, particularly if deficiencies are noted by the underwriter and need to be corrected. Finally, a day or two is required after approval for the loan documents to be prepared. Then a closing can be scheduled.[24]

---

24   MSN Money Central, http://moneycentral.msn.com/home.asp

Refinancing Your Mortgage

While most consumers focus their attention in a mortgage refinance on the opportunity to reduce their loan payments, the highest priority should be placed on reducing the interest rate and loan term. The key to creating value by refinancing your mortgage is knowing when to do it. "When" depends on a number of personal factors, so there is no simple answer. Whether or not to refinance at a given market rate may hinge upon such issues as:

1. Your current interest rate
2. The period of time you are likely to remain in your home, and
3. The size of your mortgage (the larger your mortgage, the more quickly the interest rate savings can make up for the costs of refinancing).

The cost to refinance will likely run in the range of two to three percent of the mortgage loan amount. Hence, ignoring tax effects and the time value of money (a dollar returned next year is not as valuable to you as one you have now), a one point interest rate reduction will repay the costs in two to three years. The problem is, of course, that the tax effects can be significant and the time value of money can affect the calculation as well. Hence, what preliminarily may appear to be a three-year payback, may in fact require five years.

To measure the time required to recover the cost of the refinance, consider the interest savings associated with the new loan compared to the old loan. If you are able to drop private mortgage insurance (insurance you bought to protect the lender because you made a small down payment— usually required whenever the home purchase was made with a down payment of less than 20%) from your loan by refinancing, include those savings. Some loan officers will coach you to compare the new payment to the old payment, but both payments include some principal, taxes and insurance. The comparison may be absolutely meaningless, particularly if the new loan term is significantly different from the remaining term of the original mortgage. Some financial web sites offer calculators that will help you determine your interest savings from refinancing. Consider, as an estimate, the following simple formula to determine the annual interest rate savings.

Multiply the existing interest rate on your mortgage by the current loan balance to estimate the annual interest cost. Now multiply the mortgage balance by 1.03 (to estimate the cost of the refinance) and then by the new market rate to estimate the new annual interest cost. Calculate the difference by subtracting the new annual interest cost from the existing annual interest cost. If you deducted mortgage interest last year on your tax return, multiply the difference by 1 minus your marginal tax rate.

For example:

$$((Loan \times old\ rate) - (Loan \times 1.03 \times new\ rate)) \times (1 - tax\ rate) = Annual\ Savings$$

$$(($100,000 \times .08) - ($100,000 \times 1.03 \times .06)) \times (1 - .28) = $1,310$$

In this example, it will take about 2 years and 3 months ($3,000 refinance costs / $1,310 annual savings) to recoup the costs of refinancing. If you as the homeowner are planning to be in the home for more than this amount of time with certainty, it would preliminarily appear to be a good idea.

Your loan officer will likely encourage you to refinance other debts with your first mortgage. If you roll in credit card debt or car loans into your mortgage, you'll wind up paying for your car long after it is retired. If you do have other debts, you may want to choose the mortgage refinance option with the lowest payment so that you can focus more of your cash to quickly repaying the higher rate consumer loans.

Alternatively, when rates are low, you may want to take advantage of the opportunity to not only reduce the interest rate on your loan, but to also reduce the term of the loan or amortization period. It is generally more important to reduce the rate and term than to reduce the monthly payment. By choosing a 15 or 20-year loan, your payments will be higher than refinancing with a 30-year loan in the same market, but you may find that the payments on a 15 or 20-year loan are not much higher than the payment you are making now. And you can be out of debt much sooner than with your original 30-year loan. Keep in mind, if you refinance your 30-year loan five years after you purchase your home with a new 30-year loan, you'll be paying for your home for a total of 35 years and you could actually *increase* the total interest paid to purchase the home compared to merely keeping the original loan.

Maintaining a Home

Home improvement is for some a passionate pastime. For others, it is pure punishment. The advice for one, will not work for the other.

For a passionate home improver, the only caution to consider is that while home maintenance is imperative, remodeling may not always be a good investment. The value of your home is preserved by the routine maintenance you do from cleaning to painting. On the other hand, not all home improvements improve the home.

It is important to recognize that not everyone will enjoy the lodge style, dark paneled recreation room you've built in the basement. A well-designed, professionally installed kitchen or bathroom will increase a home's value more than most home improvements. The same wouldn't hold true for the product of a casual do-it-yourselfer. Even the professional jobs may not increase the value of your home by as much as the improvements cost.[25]

Now, on the other hand, for the folks who think that cleaning the trap under the bathroom sink is a major project requiring the skills of a trained professional, you may want to consider acquiring a good guide to home repair. Such a book can guide you in the most basic plumbing and electrical tasks, allowing you to do them yourself, saving much of the cost. Be sure to start with something that is well in your range. You may even want to seek coaching from a handy neighbor.[26]

Selling your Home

Many families outgrow their homes over the years. Others move as a result of a job change or transfer. Still others move to move "up." Whatever the reason, Americans traditionally sell their homes on average every seven years. For a 35-year cycle of wedding, having and raising children and then emptying the nest, the average suggests you'll own five homes.

Each time you sell a home and buy a new one, you incur substantial transaction costs. Typically, you will pay a real estate broker a commission of 6 to 7 percent of the sales price (if you don't enlist the help of a broker, you are likely to sell the home for less, realizing the same net amount). Additionally, you will need to pay certain settlement charges, including title insurance or attorney's fees. The cost to move is also substantial, even if you do much of the work yourself. Finally, you'll likely purchase a new home and incur additional costs in that transaction, as well.

Therefore, if you can reduce the number of times you buy and sell a home, you can retain more of your wealth for missions, education and retirement. When you are trying to decide why you want to sell your home, determine whether you need to move because your home is too small or whether it is because you are looking to move up. You should also carefully evaluate whether a new home purchase, particularly if your mortgage would increase in size, fits within your current spending plan or budget. You should also evaluate the transaction in the context of your long-term financial plan.

If you have outgrown your home, you may find that finishing a basement or even constructing an addition would be cheaper in the long

25 National Association of the Remodeling Industry, "Quick Facts," www.nari.org
26 *Better Homes and Gardens Complete Guide to Home Repair Maintenance & Improvement*, James A. Hufnagel, 1980.

run than selling your home and buying a new one. The money you spend on real estate brokerage commissions is gone forever. A portion of the investment in home improvement is likely to be retained in the value of your home.

If you have the desire to move up, and the new home cost fits within your current spending plan and long-term financial plan, the key is simply to make a selection that will allow you to stay in the new home as long as possible. Evaluate the home from the standpoint of your next logical phase of life.

If you have just had your last child and she is "definitely" the last one, what if another one comes—will the new house accommodate a surprise?

If you have teenagers now, will the home work for you as empty-nesters?

If you have just retired, will your new dream home on the golf course be accessible enough for you if your mobility becomes impaired?

By eliminating two moves from your homeownership cycle, you could fund two or three missions, or 10 to 15 years of education at BYU. As you evaluate your cramped quarters or compare your modest bungalow to your brother-in-law's estate, remind yourself that owning this home, paying off the mortgage, and freeing yourself from house payments is a part of your strategy to serve the Lord and build His kingdom.

Action Items:

1. Make a thoughtful, prayerful decision with the help of knowledgeable advisors when purchasing a home.

2. Take advantage of low interest rate opportunities to refinance your mortgage in order to reduce your interest rate and the term of your loan.

3. Take good care of your home, but don't spend all of your time or money converting your home into a worldly palace.

4. Don't sell your home until you absolutely must or until a move fits readily within your current spending plan and long-term financial plan.

CHAPTER 8

FINANCING MISSIONS

And he said unto them, When I sent you without purse, and scrip, and shoes, lacked ye any thing? And they said, Nothing.

— Luke 22:35

Commitment

SERVING A MISSION without "purse, scrip and shoes" *would* require commitment. Saving for a mission both requires and creates a commitment to serve a mission. Whether the commitment is yours or your child's, a commitment must be made to serve a mission before the first dollar is set aside for that purpose. Such a commitment may in fact be little more than a hope of one day serving a mission, but it exists prior to the mission fund.

Contributing to a mission fund will increase the commitment. The commitment to serve will grow with each contribution to the fund. It is important, therefore, to get your children to contribute meaningfully to their own mission funds. By starting early, your children may be able to save a significant portion of the cost of serving a mission—even on their limited budgets.

Estimated Costs

For North American missionaries, estimating the cost of a mission is relatively easy. The Church now requires the family or ward of each missionary from North America to contribute the same amount toward the cost of the mission. For 2012, North American missionaries contribute $400 (US) each month toward the cost of the mission, regardless of the mission. So a missionary that is spending $95 per month in a rural Latin American mission is subsidizing missionaries who are serving in expensive Asian locations.

Over the last decade, the monthly assessment for missionaries has not risen with inflation; it has risen at a rate lower than inflation, suggesting that the Church has been successful in its efforts to have members donate more food and housing to help the missionaries. In planning for future missions, it is wise to anticipate some upward adjustments in the monthly mission assessment.

The following table provides an estimate of the monthly savings required to completely fund a mission by the *end* of a two-year mission. To read the table, consider the year you expect your missionary to leave and the year you'll begin to save for the mission. As you can see, if the cost of a mission is $400 per month in the year 2012 and you begin funding the mission when your missionary leaves, your monthly contribution is $400. Even though the cost of a mission is expected to increase over the years, if you start saving in the year 2012, the monthly savings requirement drops dramatically.

Year Missionary Leaves	Estimated Monthly Cost	Calculated Total Cost	Monthly Savings Required
2012	$400	$9,600	$400
2013	$405	$9,720	$262
2014	$410	$9,840	$197
2015	$415	$9,960	$158
2016	$420	$10,080	$132
2017	$425	$10,200	$113
2018	$430	$10,320	$99
2019	$435	$10,440	$88
2020	$440	$10,560	$80

Year Missionary Leaves	Estimated Monthly Cost	Calculated Total Cost	Monthly Savings Required
2021	$445	$10,680	$72
2022	$450	$10,800	$66
2023	$455	$10,920	$61
2024	$460	$11,040	$57
2025	$465	$11,160	$53
2026	$470	$11,280	$50
2027	$475	$11,400	$47
2028	$480	$11,520	$44
2029	$485	$11,640	$42
2030	$490	$11,760	$40
2031	$495	$11,880	$38
2032	$500	$12,000	$36
2033	$505	$12,120	$35

This table assumes that your monthly contributions are invested at 2% after tax.

The following table parallels the first table, but is calculated for an 18 month mission with up to 21 years to save.

Year Missionary Leaves	Estimated Monthly Cost	Calculated Total Cost	Monthly Savings Required
2012	$400	$7,200	$400
2013	$405	$7,290	$237
2014	$410	$7,380	$170
2015	$415	$7,470	$132
2016	$420	$7,560	$108
2017	$425	$7,650	$92
2018	$430	$7,740	$80
2019	$435	$7,830	$70
2020	$440	$7,920	$63

Year Missionary Leaves	Estimated Monthly Cost	Calculated Total Cost	Monthly Savings Required
2021	$445	$8,010	$57
2022	$450	$8,100	$52
2023	$455	$8,190	$48
2024	$460	$8,280	$45
2025	$465	$8,370	$42
2026	$470	$8,460	$39
2027	$475	$8,550	$36
2028	$480	$8,640	$34
2029	$485	$8,730	$33
2030	$490	$8,820	$31
2031	$495	$8,910	$29
2032	$500	$9,000	$28
2033	$505	$9,090	$27
2034	$510	$9,180	$26
2035	$515	$9,270	$24

This table is also calculated assuming a 2% after-tax return on contributions. Note also that with Sister missionaries you have two more years to save and need only save for 18 months of service.

Sharing Responsibility

As sharing in the financial responsibility for their own missions increases their commitment to serve, encourage your children to save some portion of their own estimated mission cost. Their ability to contribute will be affected by their age, the allowance you offer them, and their other sources of income. It is important to work with your children to get them to contribute a reasonable amount.

Because their income is likely to increase over the years, you may want to encourage them to contribute a fraction of their income, say 10%, to their mission funds. When they are very young, they'll contribute very little. As they get older, however, their savings will start to grow more rapidly.

Your children may find it motivational to have a target in mind. They may be willing to accept your challenge to pay for half—or more—of the cost of their mission. After evaluating what they can reasonably save and invest, you may want to help them set an appropriate goal with respect to mission savings.

Another tactic to encourage mission savings might best be described as the 401(k) tactic—match your children's contributions. If your children each set aside $10 during the month for their mission savings—match it, perhaps just fractionally (50 cents for every dollar), so that their savings will grow more quickly. In this way, you may increase their contribution and allow them to save a larger portion of the total cost of the mission, making a greater commitment to the mission.

Developing Your Missionaries' Savings Plans

Mission savings are sacred funds and should be invested that way. These are not monies that you or your child should use to speculate with. While higher return investments create the possibility of reducing your monthly savings requirements, they increase the probability of requiring you to pick up a bigger chunk of the total mission expense.

A perfectly good investment vehicle for mission savings is a passbook savings account. As the balance grows, certificates of deposit can be used. Another vehicle would be money market mutual funds; these are not FDIC insured instruments, but are generally safe. Most reputable mutual fund companies offer money market accounts that should be considered safe.

Even the most reputable mutual fund companies, however, will offer high risk sector funds or "small cap" growth funds that are not appropriate vehicles for mission savings. If you are starting the savings account before your child is baptized, you may consider some longer-term investment vehicles, such as short or intermediate term bond funds. (See chapter 14 for a more complete discussion of investment alternatives.)

Action Items:

1. Commit your children to serving a mission by starting a formal savings plan for a mission.

2. Set monthly savings goals and a target for sharing mission expenses with each child.

3. Invest the savings wisely, remembering that these funds are sacred.

CHAPTER 9

FINANCING EDUCATION

Whatever principle of intelligence we attain unto in this life, it will rise with us in the resurrection.

And if a person gains more knowledge and intelligence in this life through his diligence and obedience than another, he will have so much the advantage in the world to come.

— Doctrine and Covenants 130:18 – 19.

Fishing

MOST READERS ARE familiar with the old adage that if you give a person a fish, you feed him for a day, but if you teach him to fish, you feed him for a lifetime. Parents worry about their children being able to survive on their own in the real world. The most important economic support you can provide your children, therefore, is a quality education.

It is imperative, however, that the costs of the education be shared with your children so that they will learn self-reliance. Education should not be the first in an endless string of gifts to your young adult children, including a car, down payment on a home, or a few mortgage payments to help them get started. Learning to take care of themselves economically can help your children to develop the confidence they need to succeed in their careers, marriages, and other vital aspects of life.[27]

As previously discussed in chapter 5, regardless of how the costs are shared, it should be remembered that education is an inherently risky investment. There are no guarantees of return on investment. Hence, it is wisest to treat education like a risky business venture, funding it with adequate amounts of "equity." In business, "equity" refers to contributed owner's investments or retained earnings. Such investments are made with no guaranteed or contractual return on investment. As the business grows, however, the value of the equity grows as well. If the business fails, the debt holders have the first claim on company assets, leaving the equity investors with whatever is left—if anything.

An education is like a business in that the value of the education is uncertain until the student's career is completed 40 years later. If a student is burdened by debt, much of the increased earning potential created by the education could be required to support that debt for years after graduation. In the unfortunate circumstance where a student is unable, for health or other reasons, to complete the education the anticipated revenue may never materialize. If funded with student loans, the burden could become overwhelming without the anticipated income to pay off the debt.

Estimated Costs

The first consideration in serious planning for funding an education is to consider the cost of the education for each child and to then determine the monthly savings requirement to fully fund the education.

The following table calculates the estimated cost of four years of tuition at BYU commencing in the year indicated and the monthly savings required to fund the total four-year tuition bill, starting fall enrollments for 2012. In calculating this chart, it is assumed that the cost of tuition at BYU will rise at a rate of 4% per year (the rate at which tuition has increased, on average, over the past 13 years); the actual rate of increase could differ. The calculation of monthly savings includes contributions through the final tuition payment in the fourth year of school and presumes a 2% after-tax rate of return—which could also vary.

---

27   Thomas J. Stanley and William D. Denko, *The Millionaire Next Door*, Simon & Schuster, 1996, pp 203 –209.

Saving Plan for BYU (Estimated Costs)

Year Student Starts College	Annual Cost	Total Cost	Monthly Savings Required
2012	$4,742	$20,119	$403
2013	$4,932	$20,924	$332
2014	$5,129	$21,761	$285
2015	$5,335	$22,631	$251
2016	$5,548	$23,536	$226
2017	$5,770	$24,478	$207
2018	$6,001	$25,457	$192
2019	$6,241	$26,475	$179
2020	$6,490	$27,534	$169
2021	$6,750	$28,636	$161
2022	$7,020	$29,781	$154
2023	$7,301	$30,972	$148
2024	$7,593	$32,211	$142
2025	$7,896	$33,500	$138
2026	$8,212	$34,840	$134
2027	$8,541	$36,233	$131
2028	$8,882	$37,683	$128
2029	$9,238	$39,190	$125
2030	$9,607	$40,758	$123
2031	$9,992	$42,388	$121
2032	$10,391	$44,083	$119

The chart assumes that the four years are continuous—which may not be the case if a mission interrupts the four-year curriculum. If your student interrupts his education with a mission, you should be able to fund the tuition requirement without making regular contributions to the education fund during the mission (the interest earned in the account will approximate the inflation of the tuition—a small additional contribution will likely be required).

If your student doesn't plan to attend BYU, you may wish to compare the current cost of education at your student's target school with BYU. The ratio of current cost at the alternate school, say Harvard, to the current cost for BYU implies a multiple for the savings requirement column in the table. So, if the annual tuition cost at Harvard for 2011-2012 is $36,305, that is roughly 8 times the cost of BYU tuition of $4,560. Therefore, you should save eight times the amount indicated in the monthly savings requirement column of the BYU savings table above—for each child who plans to attend Harvard.

That said, Harvard, Princeton and some other elite colleges now admit students from families with a household income below a given threshold (Harvard's is $65,000 per year with scant financial assets) to attend at no cost. The university will even provide housing, books and a meal plan. Of course, the academic standard for admission is not reduced for such students. Families earning less than $150,000 per year but more than $65,000 may pay as little as 10% of the standard tuition cost for attending the university.

The following table compares several schools from around the country to BYU's tuition for the 2011-2012 school year and provides a range of savings multiples depending upon the school your students will attend. For each of the state schools listed, the tuition amount listed is the in-state tuition expense; out of state tuition in most cases is dramatically higher.

Cost of Tuition Relative to BYU

School	Annual Tuition	Relative to BYU
University of Utah	$6,474	x 1.4
University of North Carolina at Chapel Hill	$7,008	x 1.5
University of Texas at Austin	$10,326	x 2.3
University of Michigan at Ann Arbor	$14,246	x 3.1
University of California at Berkeley	$14,461	x 3.2
Harvard University	$36,305	x 8.0
University of Southern California	$42,818	x 9.4

The savings burden, if you already have several children, may seem overwhelming. You'll need to save the amount indicated by this process for each one of your children. Given the magic of compound interest, you'll find that it will never be easier to accomplish your objectives than it is by starting now. One other benefit will accrue to parents of multiple children—presuming that your youngest is younger than ten years old—you may invest for the longer term and take slightly more risk with an anticipated higher return. We'll discuss investment strategies in more detail in chapters 13 through 15.

It is imperative to note that the cost of room, board, books, and miscellaneous fees are excluded from the above calculations. At BYU, these costs total almost $8,000 per year, much more than tuition! That said, there are some considerations here. First, if your student is living away from home, your student isn't living at home. You should discover some benefits from not feeding another adult mouth. If your student attends a college or university close enough to home to live with you, these costs will be much lower than the cost of living on campus.

Sharing Responsibility

Room and board expenses provide a natural means for your students to contribute meaningfully to the cost of their own education. Because your student will control many of these costs, you may wish to contribute relatively little toward living expenses. If your student is required to use savings, summer jobs and even part time jobs while in school to fund living expenses, you can bet these expenses will be lower. The discipline learned through this process will also prove to be a valuable element of the overall education package your student receives.

Campus jobs paying from $7 to $10 per hour are available at most universities. These jobs provide up to 20 hours per week of work. At $8 per hour for 15 hours per week for 30 weeks of the school year, a student could earn $3,600 (which translates roughly to $3,000 after tax and tithing) for living expenses. The summer provides another opportunity for work. Over the summer, a full-time job paying $10 per hour for 12 weeks would generate another $4,800 (call it $3,000 after taxes, tithing and summer entertainment) for living expenses during the school year. In this way, a student can readily cover 50% of the living expenses from current year earnings.

For most students, particularly those who plan to serve and therefore save for a mission, their own savings are not likely to be a meaningful source of funding for a college education. Your students' contributions will likely be driven by their ability to earn a meaningful portion of their living expenses during their college years.

Sources of Financial Aid

Students may also be able to contribute to covering the cost of their own education through scholarships. In order to give your students the proper incentive to earn scholarships, you may want to commit early to awarding the tuition equivalent directly to your students if they earn scholarships that cover tuition.

BYU offers several scholarships for outstanding academic achievement. The most prestigious of which is the Gordon B. Hinckley Presidential Scholarship (renamed for each President of the Church). These scholarships cover LDS tuition plus "an additional stipend for eight semesters."[28] This scholarship requires extraordinary academic performance.

Heritage scholarships provide eight semesters of full LDS tuition based largely on academic merit. National Merit Scholarships are also eight-semester awards granted to some of the National Merit finalists from this national competition. University Scholarships of either half or full tuition must be renewed each year. Additionally, each of the colleges offers scholarships. Furthermore, there are literally dozens of family scholarships available to descendants of various wealthy benefactors. Most scholarships are awarded based largely on merit; some are granted on the basis of need.

As mentioned earlier, some elite schools now waive all expenses or significantly discount them for students from families with modest incomes. Virtually all schools will work with admitted students to find (read borrow) the money required to cover the cost of education; consider, however, the cost of accepting generous loans to attend expensive schools. The cumulative loans for entering freshmen in 2012 could reach $250,000 if all eligible expenses at expensive schools are borrowed! How would a young person ever get on top of that? It could hang over her like a dark cloud for her entire career.

In Chapter 12 you will find a complete guide to tax breaks for funding education. For the first two years of school, the Federal Government provides up to $1,500 of tax credits. For subsequent years, the credits drop to 20% of eligible expenses up to a tax credit of $1,000.

Borrowing The Balance

Once you have funded the bulk of the educational tab with a combination of equity investments (savings, student earnings, scholarships, need-based grants, etc.) you may find a small shortfall remaining. In such a case, a small amount of debt may be required to make up the difference. The Federal Government will guarantee your student loans based solely on your need. This allows you to borrow at rates typically reserved for the government (because you borrow the Federal Government's good name). In some cases, the interest during the years your student is in school will be forgiven (actually, it is paid by the Federal Government).

Because the loans are need-based, however, it is unusually easy to get the money. Here, your student is least able to pay and most able to

---

28   http://ar.byu.edu/dept_finalcial/bulletin9899/

obtain credit. This can be a dangerous combination. Your student may be tempted to borrow more than is necessary. These debts, effectively or actually owed to the Federal Government, cannot be discharged in bankruptcy. They will never go away until paid. They will hang like a noose around the neck of an imprudent student who borrows too much for his prospective income.

If you were to think of education funding like a meal, the main course should be savings. Side dishes can be counted on from current earnings, tax credits and even from some grants and scholarships (whether need or merit based, there is likely something available for your students). Finally, a small dessert of debt will go down fine. But, as with dessert after a big meal, if you have too much debt, the whole meal can be ruined by indigestion.

Action Items:

1. Save for the tuition bill of the school your students hope to attend starting today.

2. Teach your students discipline and the value of money by encouraging your students to pay as much as practical toward their own living expenses while in school.

3. Apply for every conceivable grant or scholarship—leave no stone unturned.

4. Borrow as little as possible and only if you absolutely must.

CHAPTER 10

INSURANCE

And now there began to be a great curse upon all the land because of the iniquity of the people, in which, if a man should lay his tool or his sword upon his shelf, or upon the place whither he would keep it, behold, upon the morrow, he could not find it, so great was the curse upon the land.

Wherefore every man did cleave unto that which was his own, with his hands, and would not borrow neither would he lend; and every man kept the hilt of his sword in his right hand, in the defence of his property and his own life and of his wives and children.

— Ether 14:1-2

Protect Your Plan

IN THE CURRENT day in age, it is a sad fact that financial footing can be lost due to unpredictable tragedy. These are times not substantially less risky than the days of the prophet Ether who recorded that "every man kept the hilt of his sword in his right hand, in the defence of his property and his own life and of his wives and children."

There are, however, alternatives to keeping a weapon always in hand for protecting your assets and income—even your family's health. Most of the risks that you face can wipe out even the affluent if they are inadequately insured. Generally speaking, that is why the affluent carry so much insurance.

The loss of your entire net worth can result from the same tragic car accident that robs you of a cherished family member or of your own good health. While you can't insure against the loss of a loved one, you can limit such a tragedy to a non-financial tragedy. If you lost a child, would you have any less interest in serving a mission early in retirement? If your house burned down, would you have any less desire to send your children to college? The purpose of this chapter is to help you evaluate preliminarily the available coverage to protect your financial plan. You'll certainly want to find trusted insurance advisors to help you measure your risks and cover them appropriately.

Health Insurance

There is likely no greater threat to your financial plan than health issues for you or anyone in your family. Such a problem is likely to be emotionally challenging without the added stress of financial strain. It is therefore imperative that you always maintain your health insurance coverage.

Most people obtain health insurance from their employers. In some cases, particularly with small companies, the self employed or for part-time employees, health insurance is not offered or, if it is offered, it is offered at a very high price. Sadly, there is no shortcut or secret trick. Unless you are destitute, government and charitable agencies will expect you to use virtually all of your available resources to cover uninsured medical costs. Even a minor procedure can cost thousands of dollars and wipe out years of saving for retirement.

Therefore, it is imperative that health insurance be one of your highest financial priorities.

It is also important to avoid gaps in insurance. If you are ever between jobs, be sure to take advantage of the Federal requirement (COBRA[29]) that your former employer offer you insurance for up to 18 months at a rate that is roughly comparable to its cost. This may be substantially more than you paid as an employee, but it is probably less than you'd pay for a private policy. After age 65, in the U.S. you will be covered by Medicare.

Life Insurance

Life insurance has a primary purpose of providing a death benefit to the survivors. You need to decide what that death benefit should be for each person in your family. For your children, the insured amount should be modest—enough to cover an appropriate funeral, perhaps. For a stay-at-home parent, the coverage should be enough to pay for the services

---

[29]   Consolidated Omnibus Budget Reconciliation Act commonly called "COBRA."

she (or, increasingly, he) provides until those services are no longer required as well as to cover funeral and burial costs. For the breadwinner, the calculation of the required death benefit is tricky.

First, let's review the requirement for a stay-at-home parent. Even if she doesn't work outside the home or generate income, she provides a substantial economic benefit that should be insured. She likely takes care of children, tutors them in school work, and does most of the housework. Some of these tasks could be assumed by other household members— you'll need to decide if they will be. Other tasks likely cannot be assumed by other family members due to the time required. Someone will have to be hired to replace these services until they are no longer required. For instance, day care must be provided until children are old enough to care for themselves.

So, if you believe that a funeral for the stay-at-home parent in your home would cost $10,000 and that she provides services that would require at least $5,000 per year to replace for the next ten years, you'll likely want $50,000 to $60,000 of life insurance for the stay-at-home parent.

For a breadwinner, regardless of gender, you'll want to substantially insure the income that would have been generated by the breadwinner. A simple rule of thumb is six to eight times the current annual income.[30] To determine the amount of life insurance required, you will need to consider a wide range of issues.

First, you may want to insure specific costs associated with his (or her) passing, such as the funeral or increased home-management costs that may be incurred without the help that the breadwinner provided when at home. You may also want to increase coverage to provide for missions and college education for the children. Be sure to consider your debts when determining the amount of your insurance coverage; you'll almost certainly want to be sure that all debts can be repaid from the life insurance benefits—with significant amounts left over. The number of children you have and their ages should also be a consideration; the younger they are and the more children you have, the larger the face value of your policy should be.[31]

If one spouse is at home, you may want to discuss the possibility of that spouse returning to the work force in the event of the death of the breadwinner. Planning for a stay-at-home parent returning to work does not eliminate the need for life insurance, but it can reduce it. If both spouses are already working, it is unfair to assume that the surviving spouse will

[30] Ken Dolan and Daria Dolan, "Idea of the Month/From the First Family of Personal: Our Painless 60-Minute Insurance Checkup Can Save You Money and Grief," *Money*, April 1, 1996, pp 41.
[31] Henry S. Brock, *Your Complete Guide to Money Happiness*, Legacy Publishing, 1997, pp. 248-254.

simply earn more to make up the difference. The determination of how much life insurance to buy should be made carefully and prayerfully. A trusted insurance advisor can help you calculate the insurance you'll need on the breadwinners in your home.

Be sure to take advantage of group life plans offered by your employers. You'll find that you can likely purchase coverage for less. If you have any health problems, it may be the only place you can purchase coverage. However, even if you have generous life insurance benefits at work, it is a good idea to own some insurance purchased directly through an agent. By buying some of your own insurance you are certain that in the event a tragedy occurs between jobs, there will be something there to help resolve the financial aspects of the crisis.

One of the most difficult decisions about life insurance is whether to purchase permanent (whole life or universal life that accumulates investment value) insurance or term insurance (expires worthless once you stop paying the premium). While you are young, term insurance will certainly be cheaper. Over time, term life policies become more expensive. Permanent insurance policies feature much higher premiums—but they never increase. Whole life and universal life policies also accumulate cash value that you can access. You may want to consider the cash value to be your emergency fund—don't touch it unless you are faced with a hardship that no insurance policy covers. Your insurance agent can help you evaluate the alternatives.

Disability Insurance

Most people are not aware that the breadwinner in your family is more likely to be disabled—sick or injured—for 90 days or more than he is to die. As a result of this naiveté, families are more likely to have adequate life insurance than long-term disability insurance—even though the latter may be more important to the family's financial health.

Many employers provide some disability insurance. Be sure you understand whether your employer provides such coverage, and if so, what the benefits are. Most employer-sponsored plans provide insurance for only a portion of your income, ranging from 40 to 60 percent.

You'll then need to determine whether you can live on the benefit offered by your employer's plan—if there is one. If you are near retirement and have a good retirement nest egg, you likely can get by on the insurance provided. On the other hand, if your children are about to enter college and head out on missions, it would be more important for you to insure more of your income.

You can then talk to your trusted life insurance agent about a policy to top-off the employer's plan if you have one or to cover you completely if your employer doesn't offer coverage. These private plans can be written to provide better coverage than typical employer plans. A private plan may include a clause that covers you until you can return to your exact career, called an "own-employment" policy. This compares with typical employer plans that cover your return to "any-employment" that may be related to your skills and training.

All policies, however, have some limits. Regardless of which policy you rely on, they typically do not provide any benefits past the age of 65. This is because the policies are intended to cover the income you would have earned through gainful employment before retirement—so be sure to continue saving for retirement during any disability you may experience. Another feature of the coverage is that the benefits are not indexed for inflation. If you rely on these benefits for a long period of time, the purchasing power of the benefits will decline.

Auto Insurance

As discussed in Chapter 6, reducing your investment in cars is a key element of your overall financial plan. By spending less to purchase the car, you are also likely to reduce the cost to insure it.

As with other insurance, you want to be careful to insure the risks you can't afford to absorb, but you may not want to pay to insure risks you can afford. For example, you'll want to make sure you have liability limits of at least "100/300/100" as it is often quoted. This represents a $100,000 limit for bodily injury for each person, a $300,000 limit for bodily injury for each accident (regardless of the number injured), and $100,000 for property damage. These high limits—higher than most states require—protect you against claims that are quite likely in the event of an accident.

On the other hand, there are losses you can easily absorb that you shouldn't insure. Start by evaluating your deductible. Then consider your income and available cash reserves. You may find that you are paying premiums for coverage you don't need. If you have $5,000 in your emergency fund and income well in excess of your monthly debt service, you can afford to increase your deductibles to $500 to $1,000 from the $100 to $250 that is typical on auto policies. This may offset the cost of the increased limits discussed above that you really need to protect you against the losses you can't afford.

As your cars age, you may find that you don't need collision and comprehensive insurance any more. If you've increased your deductible to $1,000 and the car is only worth $2,000, perhaps you should consider dropping the comprehensive and collision insurance altogether.[32]

Homeowner's Insurance

Your homeowner's policy is also vitally important to your financial plan—even if you don't own a home, in which case you probably need renters insurance. The policy protects your home, your belongings and also provides some limited liability insurance.

The first thing people think of when they think of homeowners insurance is fire insurance. Your policy will, of course, cover this sort of damage. The amount of coverage you need is dependent upon a wide range of variables. Consult with a trusted property insurance agent about these issues. It is most important to be sure that you have enough insurance. Your lender required you to put a policy in place—to protect its interests, not yours. As a result, you may not have enough coverage to actually rebuild your home if you purchased the minimum required by your lender. Furthermore, with building costs rising, your policy may not provide enough coverage to rebuild your home—even if the limits were appropriate once before. To be sure this coverage is in place, ask your agent about a replacement cost guaranty. Alternatively, be sure to review your coverage limits with your agent each year.

Your policy will also cover your belongings. In this regard, it is important that you have a good inventory of your belongings. Without it, you may find it difficult to make a successful claim. A video may be the most efficient means of providing an accurate inventory. If you make a video, be sure to cover every room in the house, taking valuables from cupboards and drawers. Then, upload the video (not to YouTube!) somewhere that you can access it readily after a fire. Storing it on your computer or on a tape or disk won't do much good if all that is destroyed in the fire.

Particularly valuable items will not be covered under the standard homeowner's policy without a special rider. If you have artwork, jewelry, guns or other valuable items, be sure to discuss these items with your insurance agent.

Your policy will also provide a measure of liability insurance. If the mail carrier slips on your front porch while delivering your mail, he may file suit. Regardless of whether the claim is valid, the insurance carrier will defend the suit and even pay the damages up to the limits in the policy. Your policy, however, has exclusions for business use of your home; if you work from home, you'll likely need a rider or a separate policy to cover

---

32   Sheryl Nance-Nash, "Money Newsline/Do It Now: Cut Your Car Insurance Premiums By As Much As 20%," *Money*, 2/1/96, pp. 17.

the potential liability. Furthermore, as your income and net worth grow, it is likely that the liability coverage in your policy will be too little for your circumstance; you'll want an umbrella policy (see the discussion below).

There are also a few natural hazards that are not covered by your homeowner's policy. First, a homeowner's policy never includes flood insurance. Flood insurance is only available from the National Flood Insurance Program sponsored by the Federal Emergency Management Agency. Additionally, earthquakes are typically not covered by a homeowner's policy. If you live in a coastal area prone to hurricanes, you may also find that your policy excludes hurricane damage. You'll want to buy hurricane coverage when you buy your home, because the policies usually include a short waiting period so that you don't "forget" to buy the insurance until you hear a storm is coming.[33]

Umbrella Insurance

Umbrella insurance is aptly named. Imagine an umbrella over your home, car and family protecting them all from the gaps in homeowners and car insurance. This coverage is particularly important for Latter-day Saints. Imagine yourself with a minivan full of cub scouts or a Suburban full of boy scouts. The umbrella policy will at least help you feel more confident that you can be responsible for whatever may happen.

If you've followed Church and scouting procedures, the Boy Scouts of America insurance or the Church would likely cover damages. But you could also be named personally in a lawsuit; an umbrella policy will give you some peace of mind.

Umbrella insurance policies may also include some coverage for foreign automobile accidents. If you are traveling or serving a mission abroad and are involved in an accident, the umbrella policy may cover liability arising from the accident that your automobile policy won't cover. Coverage for volunteer work or for foreign liability is not necessarily covered by all umbrella policies. Be sure to ask about these specific aspects when you purchase your policy.

As indicated above, an umbrella policy fills in gaps of your homeowners (or renters) and automobile policies. It also provides substantially higher limits. Your homeowners and automobile policies should include $300,000 of liability insurance. The deductible on your umbrella policy will also be $300,000. If there is a successful claim made against you for $500,000, your homeowners or automobile coverage would pay the first $300,000 and the last $200,000 would be absorbed by the umbrella policy.

---

[33]   Ginger Applegarth, "Homeowner's Insurance Protects More Than Your Home," Microsoft Money Central, 1/9/99. http://moneycentral.msn.com/articles/insure/property/1426.asp

Because claims are relatively rare, the policy is inexpensive. Because a claim could completely wipe out your financial plan, it is imperative.[34]

A Strong Balance Sheet

For many risks, a strong balance sheet and a cash reserve for emergencies can provide the cheapest insurance. Assuming some of the risk may also help you become a more careful driver and homeowner. Remember though, not to take risks that you cannot afford. Even if you are affluent, you can't afford to be without adequate insurance. A major illness, accident or death in your family could undo years of careful saving and planning.

The types of assets you own may also influence the risks you face. If you are driving a $10,000 car and are involved in an automobile accident, the other driver is less likely to see you as a potential windfall—deep pockets—than if you were driving a $50,000 luxury automobile. The cheaper car would also be cheaper to insure and, likely, to maintain. The same concept applies to your home. A large home on the hill can attract as much unwanted attention as it can attract compliments from friends.

As you can see, the elimination of some of the trappings of affluence can reduce your expenses and your risk of facing a lawsuit. This is also consistent with your desire to serve the Lord and to teach your children to do the same.

Action Items:

1. Carefully evaluate your insurance needs with a trusted life insurance agent, your human resources department at work, and a trusted property and casualty insurance agent.

2. Never go without coverage that you determine carefully you need.

3. Build a cash reserve for emergencies to reduce your dependence on low deductibles.

4. Don't pay for insurance to cover risks you can afford to accept.

5. Reduce your appearance of "deep pockets" in hopes of reducing your lawsuit exposure by eliminating some of the trappings of affluence.

6. Don't miss discounts available to you like good student discounts and multi-policy discounts.

---

[34]   Christine Dugas, "Insurance Can Help With Legal Bills; Umbrella Policy Gives Extra Protection," *USA Today*, 2/17/97, pp 2B.

CHAPTER 11

RETIREMENT

I shall never forget the experience we had in June of 1993 at a special meeting in Beijing, China, with couples who were then teaching English in North Vietnam and Mongolia. After two days of training and inspiration, we closed with this familiar song: "It may not be on the mountain height…" As we were singing, my wife leaned over and whispered in my ear: "But it might be 'on the mountain height,' or it might be 'over the stormy sea,' or it might be 'at the battle's front.'" The Lord surely had need for these beautiful people serving in this interesting area of the world. These wonderful missionary couples did not choose to come to these countries. Yet as we now look at the results of their service, I know that they were chosen by the Lord for their special calling.

— *Elder Monte J. Brough Of the Presidency of the Seventy,*
167th Annual General Conference,
Saturday Afternoon Session.

Planning Retirement

BEFORE YOU CAN plan financially for your retirement, you need to determine what you want to do in retirement. If you have plans to serve more than one mission abroad, your financial requirements will be quite different from someone who plans a single, twelve-month mission in the States.

Of course, you're not likely to spend your entire retirement actively serving a mission. You'll likely want to travel—perhaps with your family. You may also want a seasonal home in a warmer or cooler climate than where you have your primary residence. The two keys to achieving your financial objectives are, first, to make reasonable estimates about the cost of your plans and, second, to save enough to fund your plan.

Determining the cost of your retirement will be up to you. Work with your family and financial planner or accountant to estimate the costs of the things you want in retirement. This book will prepare you to work with them to develop a plan to achieve your objectives.

There are several reasons why you could live comfortably—not lavishly—on less income than you earn prior to retirement. First, you won't have to save for retirement after you retire. Then, once you reduce your income a bit, your tax obligation and tithing expenses also drop. If you've paid off all of your debts, you'll also have the freedom from debts that you may have been working on for 30 years. Without them, your income requirement will be lower.

Eliminate Debt

Perhaps only grandchildren can bring you more happiness in retirement than the freedom that comes from being debt free. Owning your home "free and clear" brings corollary happiness. If you own your own home and owe nothing to anyone when you retire, however modest your retirement savings may be, however small your retirement income seems, you will feel the freedom to retire and render church service.

On the other hand, if you have even a moderate amount of debt, the balance due could demand a higher income than is available from Social Security and investment income, pressuring you to work. Such a situation could preclude the opportunity to serve a mission.

As you approach retirement, it is more important than ever to begin focusing your financial planning on debt reduction. Begin by verifying the last scheduled payment of your mortgage and car payments. If any is scheduled to occur after you plan to retire, work out a plan to make extra payments to eliminate the debt before you retire. Review Chapter 5 to develop a plan to be out of debt before your retire.

Anticipating Social Security Benefits

After you work out a plan to eliminate your debt, then you can begin thinking about saving for retirement. Prior to determining your savings requirements, you need to understand what Social Security will likely provide during retirement. The formula that determines your benefits is complex, considering the number of years you've worked, the contributions you've made and your age at retirement.

As you'd expect, the more you've contributed, the more you're likely to receive. That said, assuming two people contributed to the Social Security fund for the same number of quarters and retired at the same time, the one who earned the least will receive the highest *proportion* of her pre-retirement income in social security benefits. The program is biased toward providing a minimal level of income for all participants, rather than a "fair" return on the investment.

Your retirement age will significantly impact your benefits. You may choose to retire as early as age 62. If you wait, your benefits will increase not only until you reach your full retirement age, but until you turn 70. Your full retirement age depends upon the year you were born. If you were born after 1960, your full retirement age could be as old as 67.

The best way to know your anticipated benefit is to ask the Social Security Administration to tell you. You can contact the SSA at www.ssa.gov. You'll be asked for some information that you should know—you don't need to know your historical income or contributions because the SSA has been tracking that for you. They'll send you a detailed report showing the benefit you should anticipate if you retire early, at full retirement age, or later. Most people receive a copy of this report from the SSA annually without asking.

The U.S. government imposes limits on the amount of earned income you can receive without being taxed on your Social Security benefits. The IRS sets a "base" income level, which if exceeded, subjects your social security benefits to taxation. For 2011, the base is $32,000 for married couples filing jointly and $25,000 for a single, head of household. To determine whether your income exceeds this threshold you add just half of your social security benefit to your other taxable income. The key point here is that if you've been living on an income significantly above the social security benefit level and want to maintain that income, you'll likely end up paying tax on your social security benefits.

Planning For a Comfortable Retirement

The Social Security Administration will indicate your anticipated benefit in current dollars (even though the benefit will be adjusted over the years before and after retirement for inflation). You now need to determine how much additional income you'll require—expressed in current dollars. For instance, if you'll make $100,000 this year and you'd like 80% of that in retirement, you'll want $80,000 per year of income in current dollars. If the SSA says your benefit will be $30,000 per year, you'll only need $50,000 or 50% of your current salary as income from savings.

The following table indicates the percentage of your salary that you should be saving for retirement in order to achieve a perpetual income equal to 50% of your current salary (growing to cover inflation). To use the table, you need to know only two things: 1) How many years until you plan to retire (the numbers shown in the left-hand column), and 2) the multiple of your target income you currently have in savings (the numbers shown across the top). To determine the second number simply compare your retirement savings and investments held today (say $150,000) to your target income of $50,000 by dividing the savings by the target income as follows: $150,000 ÷ $50,000 = 3. So, in the table below someone with savings equal to 3 times the retirement income goal today with 20 years left to retirement should now be saving approximately 22% of her income for retirement.

Retirement Savings Requirement

		Multiple of Desired Income Invested Today							
		0	0.5	1	3	5	7	10	12
	5	189%	183%	177%	154%	130%	107%	72%	49%
	6	154%	149%	144%	124%	104%	84%	54%	35%
	7	129%	125%	120%	103%	85%	68%	42%	25%
Years to Retirement	8	110%	106%	103%	87%	71%	56%	33%	17%
	9	96%	92%	89%	75%	61%	47%	25%	11%
	10	84%	81%	78%	65%	52%	39%	20%	7%
	11	75%	72%	69%	57%	45%	33%	15%	3%
	12	67%	64%	62%	50%	39%	28%	11%	0%
	13	61%	58%	55%	45%	34%	24%	8%	0%
	14	55%	52%	50%	40%	30%	20%	5%	0%
	15	50%	48%	45%	36%	26%	17%	3%	0%
	16	46%	44%	41%	32%	23%	14%	0%	0%

Retirement Savings Requirement

	Multiple of Desired Income Invested Today							
	0	0.5	1	3	5	7	10	12
17	42%	40%	38%	29%	20%	12%	0%	0%
18	39%	37%	35%	26%	18%	9%	0%	0%
19	36%	34%	32%	24%	16%	8%	0%	0%
20	33%	31%	29%	22%	14%	6%	0%	0%
21	31%	29%	27%	20%	12%	4%	0%	0%
22	29%	27%	25%	18%	10%	3%	0%	0%
23	27%	25%	23%	16%	9%	2%	0%	0%
24	25%	23%	22%	15%	8%	1%	0%	0%
25	24%	22%	20%	13%	6%	0%	0%	0%
26	22%	20%	19%	12%	5%	0%	0%	0%
27	21%	19%	17%	11%	4%	0%	0%	0%
28	19%	18%	16%	10%	3%	0%	0%	0%
29	18%	17%	15%	9%	2%	0%	0%	0%
30	17%	16%	14%	8%	2%	0%	0%	0%
35	13%	12%	10%	4%	0%	0%	0%	0%
40	10%	9%	7%	2%	0%	0%	0%	0%

Years to Retirement (vertical axis label)

The chart shows the savings requirement for having 50% of your earned income come from your investments in retirement. If you'd like to have more or less, you may adjust this number simply by multiplying the savings percentage number from the table by the ratio of your target percentage (say 40%) to the 50% target used in the chart (40%/50% = 80%). Hence, if you have 3 times your target income in savings and have 20 years to retirement you should save 22% of your income. However, if you only want 40% of your earned income to come from your investments, you need save only 17.6% (22% x 80% = 17.6%) of your present income for retirement.

The chart calculates your target savings by determining the nest egg that would accumulate over the years with your current salary rising with inflation (assumed to be 3%) and with your investment returns growing (tax deferred or exempt) at an average rate of 7.5% per year with annual compounding. The chart assumes that because of your obedience to the Word of Wisdom you will live a long life. In order, therefore, to protect you from inflation during retirement, it is assumed that you will need an investment account large enough to pay you your target income and still have earnings left for reinvestment so that each year your income would rise at least with the rate of inflation and you would never run out of money no matter how long you live. You would also be able to leave a substantial amount to your heirs.

The problem with the chart is that none of the assumptions will prove to be exactly correct. Whatever the inflation rate is over the next duration, it won't be precisely 3%. You almost certainly won't earn 7.5% every year on your investment portfolio—and you won't likely average that level of earnings (it could be more or less depending on your investments and the markets). To earn this rate of return may require more risk taking than you have appetite for, requiring that you save even more to invest more conservatively. That said, these are fairly reasonable guidelines and they will help you to determine a target savings rate. You should discuss your plans with your financial advisor.

As you can see from the chart, if you have a long time to go, more than 30 years, before retiring, you have plenty of time to meet your target income with a reasonable amount of savings. In fact, if you've been saving already, you may find that you have enough that with reasonable returns on investment you'd not need to save any more for retirement at all. Even if you don't need to save to reach your minimum target, it is infinitely more wise to continue saving than to start counting your chickens. A lot can happen in 20 years.

On the other hand, if you are near retirement and haven't saved a considerable amount toward your retirement already, you may not be able to save enough to reach your goal. At this point in your life, however, you may find that you are earning at your peak and that with children raised and debts paid off, you may be able to save 20 to 40% of your gross income—making retirement possible.

If retirement seems impossible on the schedule you'd hoped, consider working just one or two more years. Unless you were already planning to retire at age 70, your Social Security benefits will continue to grow, reducing your need for investment income. Furthermore, your investment portfolio will continue to grow, increasing your potential investment income. An extra year or two may just do the trick.

Strategies for Funding a Mission

To serve a mission in retirement, three things will help above all. First, you should own your home free of a mortgage (if you do have a mortgage, it should have a tiny balance relative to the value of your home and it should have small monthly payments relative to your monthly retirement income). Second, you should have all of your other debts paid off. Last, you should have enough retirement savings to generate income. If you have all three, you should have no financial trouble in serving a mission— or two.

Given that full-time missionaries can and do generally live quite frugally, you are likely to find that if you can afford to live at home, you can likely afford to live in the mission field. The only increased expense will be rent and cost of living differences associated with your field of labor (for example, it costs more to buy almost everything in London than it does in St. George, Utah). In most circumstances, your home will have a potential rental value well in excess of the rent required in the mission field to help you close the gap, if necessary.

If you've done a very good job accumulating savings, you may be able to afford to leave your home without renting it. Be sure to find someone trustworthy to watch your home. You may find that even in this circumstance you are better off renting the home to someone than merely finding a house sitter. Tenants, however little rent they may pay, may have a greater sense of stewardship than house sitters who consider the free rent a windfall.

Action Items:

1. Own your own home.
2. Plan to be debt free before retirement.
3. Save a portion of each paycheck—starting today.
4. Serve a mission.

CHAPTER 12

TAXES

And he said unto them, Render therefore unto Caesar the things which be Caesar's, and unto God the things which be God's.

— Luke 20:25

Subject to Kings

OUR TAXES ARE used for myriad purposes, from national defense to domestic welfare. Typically, citizens don't support each and every use to which the government may put our tax dollars. Our relative level of approval for the final destination of these funds does not change our obligation to pay taxes, however. James Talmage[35] clarified in *Jesus the Christ* that paying taxes is an intended part of being "subject to kings, presidents, rulers, and magistrates."[36] In essence, you could say, "we believe in paying taxes."

With that foundation, it should be noted that LDS families will typically pay less tax than non-LDS families for two primary reasons. First, tithing is deductible from income for tax calculation purposes in the U.S. Second, the IRS provides an income exemption, a tax credit for each child in the family and LDS families have the largest families on average of any religion, as evidenced by Utah's nation-leading birth rate.[37]

---

[35] James E. Talmage, *Jesus the Christ*, Ch.31, Pg.564.
[36] Articles of Faith 12.
[37] Jerry Spangler, *Deseret News*, February 2, 1997.

No single book can capture all of the personal tax situations that arise; the tax code is comprised of eight volumes. This chapter and other references to tax implications throughout this book are provided as a primer to direct further research. The observations made in this chapter have been carefully researched, but individual circumstances can significantly affect the tax implications of otherwise "basic rules." Before submitting a tax return or making investment decisions with tax implications, be sure to consult with a tax professional.

Education

Through the tax code, the U.S. Government provides substantial support and incentives to encourage education.

American Opportunity Tax Credit: Beginning with 2010, this $2,500 tax credit serves to reimburse you through a reduction in your taxes for eligible education expenses for up to four years for one student. Wonderfully, $1,000 of the tax credit is "refundable," meaning that if you owe no income tax and paid none you could get a refund of $1,000.

Lifelong Learning Credit: This tax credit provides a 20% tax credit for up to $5,000 of educational expense, therefore providing up to a $1,000 tax credit. This credit is calculated on an annual basis per tax return (married couples may not file separately and receive this credit). The impact is such that if several of your children and you are all in school at the same time, you might spend more than $5,000 on education but your tax credit is limited to $1,000. This credit may be taken for any post-secondary educational expense, including graduate school.

Traditional and Roth IRA Disbursements: Generally, withdrawals from an IRA before age 59 ½ are subject to a 10% tax penalty. Withdrawals for educational purposes from traditional and Roth IRAs (see chapter 15) are not subject to tax penalties. (Deductions from traditional IRAs will still be subject to income tax at your marginal rate.)

Student loan interest deductible: For 2010 forward, student loan interest is deductible up to $2,500 per year if your income is below $150,000 for a married couple filing jointly, or $75,000 for a single, head of household. The deduction is not limited (as it was in the past) by the number of years since the student graduated.

Most of these benefits are means tested; that is, they are available only to those who fall into modest to middle income households. The threshold varies by program and will change every year. Be sure to consult IRS Publication 970 before determining that you are not eligible. The following table summarizes the benefits and the income limitations for eligibility.

Education Related Tax Benefits

Rule	Benefit	Income Limitation
American Opportunity Tax Credit	100% of the first $2,000 plus 25% of the next $2,000 of tuition each year for the first four years of post-secondary education per student; $1,000 of which is "refundable."	For single filers, benefits are phased out between $80,000 and $90,000 adjusted gross income. For joint filers, the phase-out occurs between $160,000 and $180,000.
Lifelong Learning Credit*	20% of up to $10,000 of post-secondary tuition expenses per tax return.	For single filers, benefits are phased out between $50,000 and $60,000 adjusted gross income. For joint filers, the phase-out occurs between $100,000 and $120,000.
IRA Disbursements for Education**	Early disbursements from a Traditional IRA are subject to tax but no penalty if used for qualified Educational expense. Early disbursements from a Roth IRA are not subject to tax or penalty if used for qualified educational expenses.	None
Student Loan Interest Deductibility***	Interest on qualified student loans is deductible for five years after payments commence.	Deductions are limited for individuals with adjusted gross income over $75,000 and families with adjusted gross income $150,000.

* Ibid.
** Ibid. 2179.
** Ibid. 1005.

Children

There are two key tax breaks in the U.S. Tax Code simply for having children. The first is an income exemption that applies for each child. For 2012 the income exemption is $3,700 per child.

The second benefit is a tax credit of up to $1,000 per child. This credit is refundable, meaning that in certain circumstances, you may get a refund even if you didn't actually pay any tax. Basically, the U.S. Federal Government is paying us to have children. (As I write this, I'm temporarily living in China where families are severely penalized for having more than one child. What a contrast!) The tax credit is phased out for married couples filing jointly with adjusted gross income above $110,000 or for single, head of household filers with income above $75,000.

The Tax Code is clearly written in such a way as to make it possible for working families to be able to afford to house and raise a lot of children, including the opportunity to receive a college education.

Tithing and other Cash Contributions

Most Latter-day Saints are accustomed to taking a tax deduction for their tithing, fast offerings, mission fund contributions, etc. The effect of this deduction, for those who itemize, is that for every dollar of contributions made the donor's tax liability is reduced by a fraction of a dollar. The fraction depends upon the taxpayer's marginal tax rate. Hence, someone in the 28% tax bracket would save $28 for every $100 of offerings paid.

Having paid your offerings to the Church, in most cases all of your other charitable contributions can also be deducted. For instance, if you have paid a total of $11,600 in tithing, fast offerings and other contributions to the Church, be sure to record all of your other contributions so that you may also deduct them. Even small, casual donations (for which you receive no direct benefit) can—and should be—deducted. You should log your miles while doing Church service and deduct them. Record and obtain receipts for donations to Deseret Industries or similar organizations so that you can deduct them. As long as the non-cash donation is under $500, the IRS requires little proof of value beyond a signed receipt from the recipient.

Missions

Missionary expenses are paid directly to the Church, making them deductible if you itemize. For most LDS families supporting a missionary, there will be little difficulty in finding sufficient deductions while a missionary is out. With tithing payments—and perhaps a mortgage, the mission expenses will almost certainly allow you adequate deductions to justify itemizing.

If you itemize, for every $100 of mission expenses paid during a year, you reduce your Federal tax liability from $15.00 to $35.00 depending upon your tax bracket and subject to certain upper income limits on itemized deductions. Your state income taxes, if they have them in your state, may also be reduced by the mission payments.

Given the substantial cost of a mission, the tax deduction is quite valuable. The deduction can be worth thousands of dollars over the two-year period.

Tax Implications of Home Ownership

Owning a home can help on your taxes if you have a mortgage. The deductibility of mortgage interest encourages mortgage debt; as discussed in chapter 5, reducing total debt, including mortgage debt should be a focus of your financial plan. As long as you have a mortgage, however, be sure to deduct the interest.

You may sell your home—so long as it was your primary residence for at least two of the last five years—without paying any tax on up to $500,000 of appreciation. Losses that result from the sale of your home are not deductible from your taxable income.

Action Items:

1. Take full advantage of all of the deductions and credits to which you are honestly entitled.

2. Give generously, not just to the Church, and deduct the contributions—the IRS effectively shares the cost with you.

3. Keep good records of miscellaneous deductible expenses, such as charitable miles, during the year so that you can support your deductions at tax time.

CHAPTER 13

YOUR PERSONAL FINANCIAL PLAN

To be prudent and saving, and to use the elements in our possession for our benefit and the benefit of our fellow beings is wise and righteous; but to be slothful, wasteful, lazy and indolent, to spend our time and means for naught, is unrighteous.

— *Discourses of Brigham Young, Pg.303.*

Bringing it All Together

UP TO THIS point, we have considered each aspect of your financial plan independently. It is now time to bring the plan into focus by considering the elements of the plan in the context of the whole. The worksheet in this chapter will provide a simple vehicle for this exercise.

The nature of our over-committed lives is to spend all that we make. Relatively few have an innate ability to defer gratification by saving substantial portions of their income. Therefore, it is likely that as you work through the worksheet, you'll find that you simply don't have enough income to fund all of your commitments. Don't panic.

Fight the temptation to solve this problem with more income. You'll always find good places to spend the money you make—no matter how much you make. The key to a successful financial plan is to fund your highest priorities first and allocate your discretionary funds to the extent they may be available.

If you can't realistically make your plan work immediately, commit as much as possible to the success of the plan. Review the worksheet each time you have a change of income so that you can move toward full funding. Within three years of modest raises and good budgeting you should be fully funding your plan.

There are some things you can do to accelerate the plan. Likely problem areas will include debt service. Look closely at your lifestyle to determine whether or not there are seldom-used, valuable assets that can be sold to reduce your debt service. If you have a boat, recreational vehicle, jet skis, motorcycles or other items that get used only once or twice a year, you may be able to sell one or more to reduce your debts to bring your plan into line.

Cars are such a drain on your income that you should look closely at the little fleet in the driveway to determine if there isn't an opportunity there to reduce your monthly obligations. First, look to see if you can reduce the number of cars in the fleet. Once a car is eliminated, it takes with it the capital cost (interest on the loan or interest income foregone), depreciation, insurance, maintenance, registration fees and taxes. You'll likely even save money on fuel because it will almost certainly reduce the total number of miles driven by the fleet.

Second, you may wish to consider reducing your investment in a particular car that can't be completely eliminated. The cost of selling a used vehicle and purchasing a new one is so high, you shouldn't consider this option unless you can reduce your total monthly ownership costs by 50%. In other words, use this strategy—where appropriate—to go from owning a newer Mercedes to driving an older Dodge. Don't use this strategy to go from owning a nearly new Suburban to owning a new Dodge Durango.

In rare cases, you may even want to consider whether your home is putting a burden on your budget. It is difficult and expensive to use your home equity to fund missions, education and, worse yet, to fund retirement. Your home should provide you with a comfortable, safe place to live in a neighborhood you love. A large home is not, however, a great investment. Over the long haul, your home will appreciate at a slower rate than many other investments. Make sure that you are not over-invested in your home relative to your income and the size of your family.

Keys to Success

The long-term success of the plan will be determined primarily by two factors: 1) your ability to fund your plan by living within your budget, and 2) the success of your investments and the rate at which inflation erodes the benefits.

The first key to the success of the plan is to think of your savings and not just your tithing, taxes, insurance and debt service as absolute obligations. What is left over after funding the obligations can be spent in any way that your family sees fit. If you think of savings as what you put in the bank after funding your discretionary budget, you'll not likely be able to contribute much to savings at all.

The second key to the success of the plan is to frequently—at least annually—assess your progress. By working through the worksheet in this book every year, you'll be able to determine roughly whether you are on track or not. Therefore, if the assumptions about investment returns or inflation in the book are wrong, you can adjust your plan to compensate—if necessary. The assumptions in the book are intended to be conservative, so you may even find that you are making extra progress after a few years. Only by regularly reviewing your situation can you determine, however, whether you are ahead of the game or falling behind.

You will likely find it easier to measure your progress if you use separate accounts for each investment purpose. You'll likely use your 401(k) as your primary retirement savings vehicle if your company offers one. For various reasons, you'll want to use IRA's to fund education savings. Finally, you may find that a taxable savings or investment account is best for your mission savings. These account types will be discussed more fully in chapter 15. By using one account or set of accounts for each individual purpose, you'll better be able to measure your progress toward each savings objective.

For your convenience, the following form is also posted on-line at http://bit.ly/zJK41E in the form of a usable spreadsheet that you can download to build your own financial plan.

Financial Planning Worksheet

Line	Category	% of Income	$ (Dollar) Amount
A	Income (Chapter 2)	100%	$
B	Tithing (Chapter 4)	10%	$
C	Mission Savings (chapter 8)	%	$
D	Retirement Savings (Chapter 11)	%	$
E	Education Savings (Chapter 9)	%	$
F	Taxes (Chapter 12)	%	$
G	Insurance (Chapter 10)	%	$
H	Debt Service—Excluding Auto Loan (Chapters 5 and 7)	%	$
I	Automobile Loan/Savings Plan (Chapter 6)	%	$
J	Subtotal—Total Commitments *Enter total of lines B through I on this line.*	%	$
K	Available for Discretionary Spending (Chapter 3) *Subtract line J from line A and enter the result on this line.*	%	$
L	Total Monthly Savings: *Add lines C, D & E and enter the result on this line.*	%	$

Financial Planning Worksheet Instructions

Line A: enter the total monthly income from all available sources. Don't include any income that you can't use, like your company's 401(k) match, interest income on your IRA, etc. This will represent 100% for purposes of the worksheet.

Line B: enter your tithing amount. If you pay tithing on your net income, or if you tithe income not included in line A, you should calculate your tithing amount as a percentage of the income on line A. To calculate a percentage, divide the line B amount by the line A amount and multiply by 100. For instance, if you pay $420 per month of tithing on available income of $4,000 you would divide 420 by 4,000 and multiply by 100 to get the result 10.5%. (See chapter 4).

Line C: use the tables in chapter 8 to determine the monthly savings requirement for each of your children whom you agree plan to serve missions. Deduct any portion that your children have committed to save and use for this purpose. Enter the net amount on line C. For reference, you may wish to calculate the percentage of your income from line A.

Line D: use the table and instructions in chapter 11 to determine the percentage of your income you'd like to be saving in order to achieve your desired retirement income. For reference, you may wish to calculate the percentage of your income from line A.

Line E: use the tables and instructions from chapter 9 to determine a monthly college savings amount for each of your children. Note that if you have many children and/or modest income, it is not unreasonable to enter zero on this line. At present, tax credits will reasonably fund the bulk of the tuition expense for a college education. You can make your children responsible for the rest—many students pay their own way through college. Enter the final amount on line E. For reference, you may wish to calculate the percentage of your income from line A.

Line F: enter the total amount of taxes paid each month from your paychecks plus, if you are self employed, the amount of any quarterly estimated taxes paid (divided by three to arrive at a monthly amount). For your reference, you may wish to calculate the percentage of your income from line A. (See chapter 12.)

Line G: enter the total monthly amount of insurance premiums paid. Be sure to include health, dental, disability and life insurance premiums paid through deductions to your paycheck. Also add the monthly portion of any annual or semi-annual premiums paid for auto, life, umbrella or homeowners insurance—including amounts paid with your mortgage. For your reference, you may wish to calculate the percentage of your income from line A. (See chapter 10)

Line H: enter the total amount of your debt service as determined from chapters 5 (Debt Management) and 7 (Owning a Home). Exclude any car loans or lease payments (you'll enter those on line I). Calculate the percentage of your income from line A. If the percentage is over 35% you'll need to be thinking of an immediate strategy for reducing this line item. This can best be accomplished by selling an asset (boat, car, recreational vehicle, etc.) to reduce outstanding loan balances, but can also be accomplished through debt consolidation.

Line I: enter the amount of your automobile loans or savings plan as determined in chapter 6. Calculate the percentage of income on line A. Again, if the sum of lines H and I is greater than 40% you'll likely not have sufficient income to save according to your target. By reducing your investment in transportation, you may be able to make room in the budget for the mission, education and retirement savings you target.

Line J: enter to the sum of the line items B through I. You may also want to calculate the percentage of your income. Don't panic if on your first time through you discover that nearly—or perhaps even more than—100% of your line A income is allocated. You'll just need to develop a plan to get to your target.

Line K: enter the difference between line J and line A, calculated by subtracting line J from line A. This is the money you can budget according to the instructions in chapter 3. For your reference, you may wish to calculate the percentage of income on line A.

Line L: enter the sum or total of lines C, D and E. This represents the total amount that you should be putting into longer-term savings for specific purposes: mission savings, retirement savings and education savings. In addition, once your cars are paid off, you'll be making your car payments to yourself and those dollars can be added here as additional savings. For your reference, you may wish to calculate the percentage of income on line A.

Is It Too Late? An Accelerated, 10-Year Financial Plan for Those Nearer Retirement

If you find yourself in the position of being near retirement with little savings, you will need to work out an accelerated plan. For purposes of this discussion, let's presume that you are between the ages of 55 and 60 and are willing to work for another 10 years. (If you prefer to work until you physically/mentally cannot, you'll likely need a great deal less savings—focus on eliminating debt and when you finally have to quit work, your home can be your primary source of income.)

Step 1. Assess your circumstances. Apart from retirement what major obligations do you have left? How many of your children have yet to serve missions? … go to college? Determine, using the worksheet what you should be doing. If you discover that you are on track, just keep up the good work. Otherwise, proceed to step 2.

Step 2. Reduce your obligations. Look for all realistic opportunities to reduce your obligations.

Will your teenagers accept more responsibility for funding their own missions? What about education? If they balk, ask them if they'd prefer to pay for your retirement! Also assess your investment in a home.

If your home is bigger than you need because some—or all—of your children have left home, can you sell it and purchase a less expensive home or condominium that will suit you in retirement? Whatever you do with your home, be sure that your mortgage will be paid off within ten years. If you sell your big home and buy a new one, get a ten-year mortgage. Make sure that you can pay off all of your existing debt within the ten years you plan to work.

Also look at your fleet of cars. If you have had teenagers at home, you may have several cars. How many do you really need? Is there a bus that could take your teenagers to school? Can you take them on the way to work? Also consider the size of the investment in each car. If you have expensive, nearly-new vehicles, can you sell one and buy a much cheaper car? Don't sell a car and buy a new one for the sake of a small difference in investment and operating costs—shoot for halving your monthly ownership costs or don't trade down.

Among all of the assets you may be able to liquidate, you may be able to either substantially reduce your debts or fund an initial contribution to a retirement savings plan—or both.

Step 3. Reassess your circumstances. Using the worksheet in this chapter, determine whether after making the adjustments above, you can fund your target plan fully with just ten years to go. If so, you're done. Otherwise, continue with Step 4.

Step 4. Adjust your retirement income target. The retirement savings tables in this book are intended to provide you with a steadily increasing income during retirement because you should be spending less than the total income generated by your savings each year. This should result in your savings—and income—growing each year. It also means that when you die, there will be a tidy estate left over.

With just ten years to retirement, you simply may not be able to save enough to fund that sort of retirement. If you save half as much and initially spend the same, you'll spend a little bit of your principal each year until after 17 or 18 years, you'll have nothing left in savings. At that point, you can use the value of your home to fund your remaining years of retirement. You may also determine that you can live on less income than you had hoped to enjoy in retirement, further reducing the savings target.

Step 5. Final assessment. Using the adjusted savings requirement from Step 4, use the worksheet in this chapter one more time to see if you can make your financial plan work. If not, you should be much closer than when you started. Work at the plan for a year and then update your worksheet.

Additional Help

Regardless of your circumstance, it is wise to discuss your plans with your financial advisors. These could include a good tax accountant, a trustworthy casualty insurance agent, a certified life insurance agent, and an investment advisor.

For your particular circumstance, they should be able to help you adjust this plan to better suit your particular objectives. If your advisors are not LDS, and there is no reason that they should be, be very clear in explaining your objectives, particularly as respects your mission savings plans.

Action Items:

1. Use the worksheet in this chapter to put together a simple plan; seek advice from your financial advisors to personalize the plan.

2. Open appropriate savings and investment accounts immediately —if you haven't already done so.

3. Begin funding your monthly contributions to mission, retirement and education savings accounts.

CHAPTER 14

INVESTMENT ALTERNATIVES

If you wish to get rich, save what you get. A fool can earn money; but it takes a wise man to save and dispose of it to his own advantage.

— Discourses of Brigham Young, Pg.292.

Introduction to Investing

BEFORE READING THIS chapter, it is important for you to understand what it will and won't do. First, it will provide a simple overview of the investment landscape, giving you a sense of your investment alternatives. On the other hand, it won't prepare you to make your own investment decisions, it won't teach you strategies for "day trading" stocks or getting rich in the stock market.

For many years, investing was the private purview of well-moneyed individuals and institutions. Regular folks began thinking about investing in the late 70's and early 80's when Fidelity's Magellan Fund year-after-year achieved investment gains and grew to be the largest mutual fund in America. At the same time, many corporations began eliminating traditional pension plans and replacing them with defined contribution plans known as 401(k) plans (named for the IRS code section that created them). These new plans allowed the participants to make some of their own investment decisions.

Today, many small investors make their own investment decisions. Nonetheless, many people who are actively trading securities lack the formal training and experience that professional traders have traditionally enjoyed. For many, investing in the stock market has become something akin to gambling. True investing involves the mitigation of risk through diversification. By purchasing a portfolio of investments, the probability of going broke is dramatically reduced.

On the other hand, the prospect of losing all your chips is very real when the investor bets the whole stack on a few volatile investments. Some, sadly, go so far as to make such outrageous bets with borrowed money[38]. This may be the surest way to financial ruin.

Stocks

For many people, stocks are the first type of investment considered when saving for retirement. The reason is really quite simple: over the long haul, returns on stocks generally outperform the returns on other investment assets.

Before discussing the appropriateness of stock market investing in general, it is important to establish a clear understanding of what stocks are. Owning stock or shares of stock in a corporation is a simple, limited-risk means to own a share or portion of a corporation.[39] As a stockholder, your liability is limited to your investment. The corporation cannot force you to contribute more money to cover operating risks. Your share of ownership, your stock, may become worthless, but that is the limit of your risk.

Individual stocks may become intrinsically more valuable over time if the company grows in size, particularly as measured by sales and earnings. Stock market prices are determined moment by moment throughout the day by computers (in the olden days, that is the 1990s and before, market makers or specialists) that accept both "buy" and "sell" orders by maintaining a portfolio of shares in the issues in which they make a market or specialize. At any given moment, several people are willing to buy and several are willing to sell the same stock, each at a price. Some market participants will accept the market price, others set limits. When more shares are for sale than the market is willing to buy at a given price, the price tends to fall until more buyers are drawn into the market by the apparent bargain. Conversely, stock prices rise when there are more buyers than sellers in the market.

---

38   Matthew Schifrin, "Amateur hour on Wall Street," *Forbes*, January 25, 1999, cover story.
39   John Downes, Jordan Elliot Goodman, *Barron's Dictionary of Finance and Investment Terms*, Barron's Educational Series, 1991, p. 435.

The result of this market system is that stocks are generally fairly priced. Occasionally, however, stocks may be over or under valued. Such mispricing creates an added level of risk. What if you buy when a stock is overvalued because everyone is talking about the stock? What if you sell when it seems that everyone is dumping a troubled stock? Even professionals don't know what a stock's price will do in the future, creating the possibility that you could buy or sell at the wrong time. It seems that even the most naïve stock investors understand the old adage, "buy low, sell high" but many seem to buy high and sell low.

The best way for most investors to own stocks is through mutual funds (discussed later in the chapter). If you prefer to own stocks directly, there are two fundamental strategies that help reduce the risks of stock ownership. First is the tried-and-true buy-and-hold strategy. If you have a lump of cash to invest, you may wish to invest a portion in the stock market, with good advice from qualified professionals. Once you make an investment, hold the stocks for a long time. Formally review the performance of the portfolio on a periodic basis—no less frequently than annually and no more frequently than monthly. At each review, consider whether the stocks you own continue to meet the objectives you had in mind when you purchased them. As a general rule, be patient.[40]

The second strategy for reducing risk in the stock market is to use dollar cost averaging. If you make an investment of a fixed dollar amount each month—as opposed to lump sums periodically when you think the timing is just right—you can smooth some of the highs and lows out of your portfolio. By making a fixed dollar investment each month (or quarter or year) in a particular security or set of securities, you buy more shares when they are cheap and fewer when they are relatively expensive. Dollar cost averaging is easy within a 401(k) plan where contributions are deducted from your paycheck. You can accomplish the same thing, however, with a bit of discipline and any investment account. Keep in mind that dollar cost averaging does not eliminate the risk of stock ownership, but it does tend to smooth out the bumps.[41]

Bonds

Another investment alternative, one that is generally considered more conservative than stocks, is bonds. There are all sorts of bonds with widely varying investment profiles, but all have one thing in common: a bond represents an entity's promise to repay a debt. When you buy bonds, you become a lender.[42]

---

[40]   Don Underwood, Paul B. Brown, *Grow Rich Slowly*, Viking, 1993, p. 265.
[41]   Ibid, pp. 227-233.
[42]   John Downes, Jordan Elliot Goodman, *Barron's Dictionary of Finance and Investment Terms*,

As a lender, you should be concerned about the creditworthiness of your borrower. When you buy Treasury bonds issued by the Federal Government, you can be confident that your money will be returned—with interest. At the other end of the spectrum, when you purchase high yield or junk bonds (the issuers don't like to call them junk) you'll typically receive a higher interest or coupon rate, but you may not be able to collect all the money. In between these extremes there are bonds of every sort, from Government Agency and Municipal bonds, to investment grade corporate bonds.

There are three rating agencies that evaluate the credit risk of corporate and municipal bonds. Before buying a bond you'll want to understand the ratings assigned by Standard and Poor's, Moody's Investors Service or Fitch's Investors Service. Ratings range from AAA, the strongest rating, to D, when the issuer is in default.[43]

Such ratings, however, have proven to be less reliable in recent years than previously believed. Hundreds of billions of dollars worth of triple A-rated bonds defaulted and paid out nothing as the sub-prime mortgage lending market completely unraveled in 2008.

An echo of that calamity is likely to be heard in the municipal bond market in coming years as cities around the country discover that they cannot meet their obligations. Be sure to scrutinize municipal bond investments for credit risk just as you would corporate bonds.

Bonds are typically sold in units of $1,000 (except municipal bonds, which are sold in $5,000 units). That said, a $1,000 bond with a 5% coupon rate[44] will sell for less than $1,000 (or "at a discount") if prevailing interest rates for like securities are higher; conversely, if rates are lower, the bond will sell for more than $1,000 (or "at a premium"). Your total return on investment, therefore, is not the coupon rate, but instead must be calculated. Your return is a function of what you paid for the bond, the interest received over the period you own the bond, and the amount you actually receive at maturity or when you sell the bond.

Even the most credit worthy bonds carry interest rate risk. The longer the term of the bond, the greater its sensitivity to interest rate fluctuations. A 30-year treasury bond carries much more interest rate risk than a five-year corporate bond. Large interest rate swings can cause a bond portfolio to lose a 5 to 10% of its value—potentially more. In 1994, for instance, interest rates rose dramatically, resulting in some bond portfolios reporting

---

Barron's Educational Series, 1991, p. 42.

[43]   Ibid, p. 44.

[44]   Prior to the universal use of computers, bonds were sold with coupons attached that could be redeemed for an interest payment; today, bond ownership is registered in a computer and the interest is deposited into your brokerage account or checking account.

losses for the entire year—even after taking into account the interest paid on the bonds during the year.

One strategy for owning bonds as you approach retirement is to "ladder" them, that is, to stagger the maturities so that each bond matures at a different time. In this way, you reduce some of the interest rate risk because you won't have to reinvest all of the money at the same time. When each bond matures, rates will vary—sometimes higher, sometimes lower. Remember, if rates go way up and you'd like to reinvest to take advantage, the bonds already in your portfolio will have gone down in value so you'd have less to invest. You are likely better off to hold the bonds until maturity and avoid the transaction expense.

Money Market Instruments

Money market instruments typically include investments that do not fluctuate in value, but return an agreed-upon rate of interest over a short period. True money market instruments include, negotiable certificates of deposit (CDs), Treasury bills (U.S. Treasury debt with maturities of less than one year), commercial paper (essentially very short-term corporate bonds), and overnight borrowing and lending between banks.[45]

Small investors usually access these sorts of investments indirectly through a bank deposit or a money market mutual fund (more on funds later). In this way, your savings earn a money market rate of interest and you generally have access to your money. CDs present an exception to the rule in that your access to the cash deposited is not accessible until maturity. Short-term CDs, say less than a year, can practically be considered money market investments. Longer-term CDs are something of a hybrid instrument, more like a bond investment in some respects.

While many investors consider money market instruments to be safe investments because there is typically no credit risk—you always get your money back with interest—there is a substantial risk associated with money market investing. Over the long term, money market instruments pay an interest rate that only modestly exceeds the inflation rate. As of 2012 and for the last several years, money market returns have not even kept up with inflation, with returns hovering around 1%. This means that money invested in money market funds may not be worth as much in the future—even with accrued interest—as when you put the funds into savings. On an after tax basis, in the long run these investments likely will not even keep up with inflation.

All things considered, therefore, you will probably want to invest only a portion of your savings in money market-type instruments. If, however,

---

[45]   Ibid, p. 258.

you can't sleep at night if some of your assets are invested in stocks and bonds because you never know how much they'll be worth in the morning, just plan on significantly increasing your savings rate to adjust your plan. In very rough terms, if you limit yourself to these conservative investments, you'll need to double your savings rate to achieve the same level of future income you'd get with a portfolio comprising mostly stocks and bonds.

Mutual Funds

Mutual funds are professionally managed portfolios of stocks, bonds or other market securities. A mutual fund offers small investors a better opportunity to diversify a small portfolio than is otherwise practical. A typical fund owns hundreds of securities—unless you are a full-time investor with millions of dollars, it would be impractical for you to follow and analyze so many companies.

Mutual funds are an inexpensive means to get professional investment advice. Again, unless you have a large portfolio, you would likely find it unprofitably expensive to hire a private investment manager. But you can get the same sort of investment help simply by investing in mutual funds.

The sad truth, however, is that relatively few stock funds outperform the market in general. Mutual funds can also lose money—just like the stocks and bonds they buy. Therefore, even though a mutual fund offers instant diversification, it is a good idea to spread your money around, putting money in several funds from various investment companies with individual fund managers and distinct objectives.

You may want to invest a small portion of your portfolio in an aggressive growth fund that invests primarily in small, rapidly growing companies to provide some rapid growth opportunities to your portfolio. You may wish to add a fund that invests in large companies; this sort of fund will provide good long-term growth potential with a bit of current dividend income. You could also add a fund that invests in preferred stocks, high yield bonds or dividend paying common stock; some such funds offer some growth potential and some current income.

You can also invest in bond funds of all sorts. You'll find bond funds that focus on either Federal government bonds, municipal bonds or corporate bonds. These funds can also be divided into funds with long, intermediate or short-term investments.

Finally, money market mutual funds are appropriate places to keep a portion of your investments for the long term. Unlike other funds that have prices that fluctuate every day like the stock market or the bond market, money market mutual funds are denominated in shares worth one dollar. The interest rate varies, but the value of your principal remains constant. There is, however, a small risk of default with no federal deposit insurance to back up these investments so never put all of your money in one single money market fund.

Most small investors will find that their best investment options include a substantial investment in mutual funds. Even larger investors may find that mutual funds offer portfolio diversification that cannot be achieved in any other way; ten different funds will offer you ten different fund managers and thousands of underlying investments.

Risk and Diversification

The following chart compares the standard deviation (a measure of risk) with the return on 10 different types of mutual funds. As you can see in the chart, in most cases the greater the standard deviation the greater the average return.

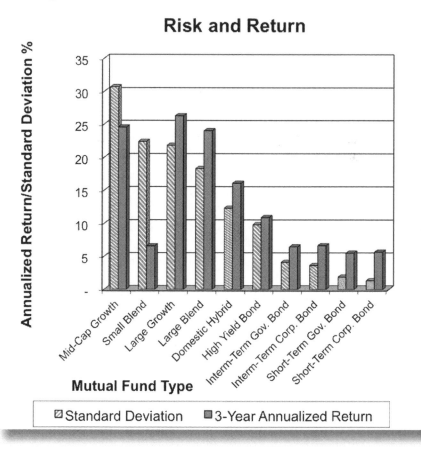

The standard deviation represents the average variation in return computed using three years of data. The return calculation is also based on three years of data.[46] The chart demonstrates the risk associated with having all of your investments concentrated in higher risk categories—the time when you need the money may not correspond with the time when the assets are at their highest value. On the other hand, the chart also demonstrates the risk of having all of your investments in lower risk accounts—their average annual returns simply aren't high enough.

Hence, the need to diversify your investments by owning a range of assets, including some from higher and lower risk categories. Your personal risk tolerance level should be discussed with your investment advisors so that together you create a portfolio with the performance you want with a level of risk you can tolerate.

Day-Trading, Derivatives and Other Folly

The Internet provides investors with a level and quality of information that only a few years ago was the purview only of stockbrokers and institutional investors. This new flood of information has convinced millions of Americans that empowered with the same information as the big boys, they are now capable of using the same sophisticated investment strategies. Some have quit jobs to become full-time day traders. Others have borrowed money—in violation of securities laws—to invest in the stock market.

This is not investing. This is not financial planning. This is financial folly. Many of these investment strategies have negative expected returns. Take option trading, for example. Options require two parties to accept equal, but offsetting positions with respect to an underlying instrument, say IBM stock. Therefore, when one party wins, the other party loses. Options (futures, swaps and most other derivative securities feature the same result) are a zero sum game and the middle man is the only one with a guaranteed position—a commission. The other parties, on average, expect to lose a little bit. There are two sorts of people who trade options: first, those who have a business or investment need to hedge an existing business risk and, second, speculators or gamblers.

You, almost certainly, do not have an investment risk that needs to be hedged and you almost certainly lack the training required to measure such risk—it is not something that a typical stockbroker could calculate for you, either. Speculation, furthermore, is not investing—it's gambling.

If you have a hankering for actively trading stocks or derivative securities, try it on paper for a while. Most people will see that actively

---

[46]   Microsoft Investor, http//investor.msn.com, March 11, 1999.

following the markets is difficult work. Regardless of how much time you might spend managing your fictional portfolio, you'll rarely beat the returns you'd have earned with a much lower risk strategy of buying and holding investments with the added power of dollar cost averaging.

If small investors could regularly beat the markets, the typical mutual fund—run by a team of professional investors with more training and time than you can imagine—would always beat the return of the market. In fact, however, year after year, most funds lag the broad market indices because markets are too hard to predict.

Action Items:

1. Find an investment advisor that you can trust.
2. Develop an investment plan appropriate for your risk profile.
3. Commit your existing savings to the plan.
4. Contribute regularly to the plan.

CHAPTER 15

INVESTMENT ACCOUNTS

I see men who earn four, five, ten or fifteen dollars a day and spend every dime of it. Such men spend their means foolishly, they waste it instead of taking care of it. They do not know what to do with it, and they seem to fear that it will burn their pockets, and they get rid of it. If you get a dollar, sovereign, half-eagle or eagle, and are afraid it will burn your pockets, put it into a safe. It will not burn anything there, and you will not be forced to spend, spend, spend as you do now.

— Discourses of Brigham Young, Pg.180 - Pg.181.

Where to Keep Your Investments

PUTTING YOUR INVESTMENTS in the right sort of account or vehicle is almost as important as the investment choices themselves. Because many forms of retirement—and other savings accounts—are tax advantaged (i.e., tax deferred, tax deductible or tax exempt) you can substantially increase your after-tax return on investment by using an appropriate account.

As can be seen in the following graph, a tax-deferred or tax-exempt account will grow more rapidly because the returns can be reinvested each year without having to pay taxes in the current year. After 25 years, the tax-deferred account has better than 40% more than the taxable account. In this chapter two general types of tax-advantaged accounts will be described—401(k) employer sponsored retirement plans and Individual Retirement Accounts or IRA's.

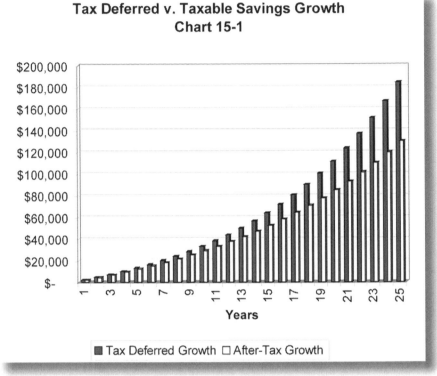

Tax Deferred v. Taxable Savings Growth
Chart 15-1

The chart assumes that $2,000 per year is contributed and invested at a 9% before-tax return. Using an assumed marginal tax rate on investments of 25%, the taxable account grows more slowly than the tax-deferred account.

There are some good, strategic reasons to have an assortment of accounts. Each is subject to contribution and withdrawal limits under certain circumstances. Therefore, you likely need one or more tax-advantaged savings accounts for retirement and education expenses and at least one long-term savings account that is subject to tax for auto purchases, mission expenses, emergencies and other expenses that cannot be funded from an IRA or that are tax deductible.

Employer Sponsored 401(k) Plans

Today, one of the most common investment accounts available to most employees, is the employer sponsored defined contribution 401(k) plan. This plan is named for the section of the IRS code that enabled this type of plan.

This plan is fundamentally a deferred compensation plan. The portion of your income that you defer, by contributing to the plan is then deducted from your current year wages—but the money you contribute is still yours. Furthermore, the interest, dividends and capital gains that accrue within the plan continue to grow tax deferred until you withdraw the funds in retirement.

The tax deductibility of the plan makes it affordable to contribute. For instance, if you contribute $100 per pay period to the plan, the taxes deducted from your paycheck will also be reduced. The amount of the tax savings depends on your marginal tax rate. Your combined State and Federal marginal tax rate could easily approach 30 to 40%—depending upon where you live and how much you earn. Assuming a combined marginal rate of 35%, a $100 contribution will only cost you $65 after tax.

Your employer may match, or partially match, some or all of your contribution. The taxes on the match are also deferred until you withdraw the funds in retirement. Typically, you will not have immediate ownership of the matched funds; there is a vesting schedule, typically two to five years—over which time the matched funds truly become yours. If you leave before the vesting schedule is completed, you'll forfeit some of the match—but you always keep the funds you contributed plus the interest and gains on your money.

You will typically have the option to contribute up to 100% of your salary to the 401(k) plan up to $50,000 (for 2012). The limit increases roughly with inflation. The company's match *does* count toward your total dollar contribution limit.

There are some strict rules that govern pre-retirement access to the funds either as a hardship disbursement or as a loan. You won't want to touch these funds, however, until you are retired. Don't think of your retirement savings as a convenient source for money for major purchases or speculative investments. This money should be treated as sacred because it can provide you the means to retire while you are still healthy enough to serve a mission.

In order to determine how much to contribute to the fund, start by identifying your target savings rate using the table in Chapter 11. You'll also want to consider the employer's match. (If you don't expect to stay with your employer long enough to fully vest, you should probably ignore the match in this determination.) If the match is, for instance, 50% of the first six percent of your salary you contribute, then a six percent contribution yields a 9% savings rate (6% + 3% = 9%) for purposes of the

Table in Chapter 11. If your target savings rate is ten percent, then you would contribute 7% to the plan. With the three-percent match from your employer, you've reached your goal.

Don't pass up free money! In the unusual, but wonderful circumstance that your employer's match is very generous, you should contribute enough to take advantage of the full match—even if it exceeds your target savings rate. For instance, if your employer matches 100% of the first six percent and your target savings rate is 10%, you could contribute just five percent and reach your 10% target. On the other hand, if you contribute the extra 1% to get the full match, you will accomplish three desirable objectives: 1) you will defer more income tax 2) your employer will give you more money for the same amount of work 3) you'll accelerate your savings plan.

Individual Retirement Arrangements (IRAs)

There are a host of different IRA account options available to investors today. It is beyond the scope of this document to consider all of the options and nuances associated with each. This section will provide, however, an overview of traditional IRA accounts and the Roth IRA introduced in 1998.

Traditional IRA. The traditional IRA is a tax-deductible plan that is self-administered. The contributions to the IRA are, however, only deductible if you are an employee (you are earning income and you are not self-employed) and are not covered by a qualified retirement plan. For 2011, there is a $5,000 per year limit ($6,000 for those over 50) on your contributions to a traditional IRA. You may also contribute $5,000 for a working spouse ($6,000 for those over 50).

Provided that you meet the requirements, you may deduct your contribution to the Traditional IRA. Hence, the $10,000 contribution would cost you only $6,500 if your combined State and Federal marginal tax rate were 35%.

When you retire, you will be taxed on the funds you withdraw from the account. It will be treated as regular income regardless of how the income or gains accumulated: dividends, interest, capital gains, etc. (So be sure not to put any tax advantaged assets, i.e., municipal bonds, into the account because you'll lose the benefit when you withdraw the funds.) To make sure that the taxman gets his due, the IRS requires you to make distributions from your IRA after age 70.

Generally, if you withdraw funds from your IRA before age 59 ½ (55 with certain provisions) you will have to pay tax on the withdrawal plus a 10% penalty. One key advantage of the Traditional IRA is that educational expenses for you, your spouse or your children can be paid with funds from your IRA. The funds are taxable but no 10% penalty will apply. You can also use up to $10,000 from this account for a first-time home purchase.[47]

Roth IRA. The Roth IRA is a non-deductible, tax exempt account. That is to say that the funds you contribute cannot be deducted on your current year's tax return, but when you withdraw the funds they won't be taxed—at all. One big advantage of Roth IRAs is that you can contribute to a Roth even if you are covered by a qualified retirement plan through your employer, such as by a 401(k) plan. You cannot, however, contribute to both a Traditional IRA and a Roth, even if you are not covered by a qualified retirement plan.[48]

Some people wonder whether they should invest in a Traditional IRA or a Roth IRA. If you are in a situation where you can deduct your contributions to a Traditional IRA, you'll want to consult with a tax advisor to determine which would be best for your particular situation.

The Roth IRA effectively allows you to contribute more than a Traditional IRA. A $5,000 contribution to a Roth IRA is worth more in the future than a $5,000 contribution to a Traditional IRA, but it costs you more today. The reason for this relationship is the difference in the tax treatment of the contributions and withdrawals. Traditional IRA contributions are deductible in the year of the contribution and withdrawals are taxed when distributed. On the other hand, Roth IRA contributions are not deductible and the withdrawals are not taxed when distributed.

In order to avoid tax at the time of distribution, you must have the funds invested for five years and then meet one of four tests: the distribution must be made after you turn 59 ½, after your death, after suffering a disability or for the down payment for the purchase of a first home. Another advantage of the Roth IRA over the Traditional IRA is that the IRS never requires you to start taking withdrawals and you can make contributions as long as you have earned income. [49]

Self Employment Retirement Accounts

There are more self employment retirement options available than there are for the employed. They are also somewhat more complex.

Savings Incentive Match PLan for Employees (SIMPLE) Retirement Plans: These plans are specifically intended for small employers and may take the form of an IRA plan. The employer is required to make a contribution

---

47   Ibid, pp. 509-514.
48   Ibid, pp.514-515.
49   Ginger Applegarth, "How to Choose Between an IRA and a Roth IRA," Microsoft Money Insider, Sept. 21, 1998, http://moneyinsider.msn.com/content/lookingahead/retirement/CV43.asp.

to the account of each employee, either 3% of compensation as a match or 2% regardless of whether the employee participates. The owner(s) of the company may participate. Each employee, including the owner, may contribute as well. The employee contribution cannot exceed $11,500 in 2012. In any case, the employer may not offer any other qualified retirement plan. All employees who earn more than $5,000 must be eligible to participate. This plan is most effective for employers who wish to provide some retirement benefit to their employees as well.

Taxable Accounts

As mentioned at the outset of this chapter, there is good reason not to have all of your money invested in tax-advantaged accounts. The primary reason is that you may want to get at your money at a time that does not coincide with the IRS's predetermined opportunities for accessing your money without penalty. Another reason is that some assets are themselves tax advantaged and as a result require no special account for their deposit. Finally, some of the purposes for which you'll put your money to use are tax deductible and therefore, may not require tax-advantaged growth.

There are several purposes for which you will want to have money growing without the constraints of retirement oriented accounts. Your new car fund—which should be relatively large and growing—is not covered by any IRS tax preference scheme. You will almost certainly want to buy a car again before your retire. Your emergency fund should also be available to you without penalty at any time. Your operating cushion, the funds you keep in reserve for non-emergency, discretionary purchases should also be readily available without penalty. These three special purpose accounts, at least, are best held in traditional, non-tax-advantaged accounts.

As you will remember from the last chapter, municipal bond interest payments are not subject to Federal income tax and most States also don't tax interest on their own bonds. A municipal bond is said to be "double tax-free" when it is owned by someone paying taxes in the state that issued it. Furthermore, growth in the value of a stock is not taxed until the stock is sold and the gain is realized. Then it is subject to a lower tax, called capital gains tax, than your standard income. (Caution: capital gains tax rates are a political issue and change more often and more significantly than other tax rates. It is possible that you could buy an asset today expecting to sell the appreciated asset at a gain later, anticipating a favorable tax rate that may not be available in the future.) This creates an argument for holding some of your stock positions for a very long time in taxable accounts. By holding such a security over a span of decades and then paying only the capital gains tax at the end, you'll actually do better than holding the same asset in a retirement account.

Another consideration is tax deductibility of the expense to which the funds will be put. The best examples of this are tithing and mission funds. If you have held individual, appreciated stocks over a long period of time, there are substantial tax savings available for using these assets to pay tithing or mission expenses directly. This benefit is not available if you hold the assets in an IRA or 401(k) plan. The benefit accrues thus: if you pay your tithing with appreciated stock, the IRS does not require you to recognize or pay tax on the gain, but you may fully deduct the value of the asset. So, suppose you pay $5,000 of tithing in the form of 100 shares of $50 stock that you purchase for $10 per share. You get a tax deduction for $5,000, credit with the Church for having paid $5,000 of tithing, and you don't have to recognize $4,000 of gains.

Therefore, be sure to keep some of your assets in regular, taxable accounts. This requires a bit more discipline because the funds are more readily available than is the case for other tax-advantaged accounts. By their restricted nature, IRAs and other tax-deferred accounts impose a savings discipline on you.

Trusts

Entire books have been devoted to the subject of trusts. Attorneys and other professionals specialize in setting up these legal entities for various purposes, from optimizing the management of assets during retirement with revocable living trusts to reducing inheritance tax with generation skipping trusts. The only type of trust that falls within the scope of this book is the Charitable Trust. At that, only an overview will be provided. If this mechanism for leaving part or all of your assets to the Church or other charity appeals to you, seek the advice of an attorney who specializes in this field.

Although there are several types of charitable trusts, an outline of the Charitable Remainder Trust will be provided in order to give the reader some idea about what can be accomplished with a trust.

The Charitable Remainder Trust is particularly appealing if you have successfully created a retirement portfolio adequate to create a perpetual retirement. Think of it this way: if your retirement funds exceed 20 times your current annual income retirement, this plan can work well for you.

With help from your attorney, you can contribute all of your retirement funds to a Charitable Remainder Trust and immediately receive a tax deduction equal to the estimated present value of the gift that will ultimately go to the beneficiary. You can also receive a benefit of 5% (1/20th) or more of the balance each year until you die. Properly invested, this could create a slowly growing retirement income—one that could keep up with inflation. After you and your spouse die, the money goes to the Church and/or whatever other charities you designate.

Action Items:

1. Create a diversified retirement account structure using a combination of tax-advantaged and taxable accounts.
2. Contribute regularly to the accounts.
3. Be particularly careful not to buy and sell assets frequently in your taxable accounts.
4. At retirement, evaluate whether a Charitable Remainder Trust is right for your situation.

CHAPTER 16

MEASURING SUCCESS

When one puts business or pleasure above his home, he that moment starts on the down grade to soul ruin. The loss of fortune is nothing compared with the loss of home. When the club becomes more attractive to any man than his home, it is time for him to confess in bitter shame that he has failed to measure up to the supreme opportunity of his life and has flunked in the final test of true manhood. No other success can compensate for failure in the home. This is the one thing of limitless potentialities on earth. The poorest shack of a home in which love prevails over a united family is of greater value to God and future humanity than the richest bank on earth. In such a home God can work miracles and will work miracles.

— David O. McKay, General Conference, April 1935

Count Your Blessings

AS YOU APPROACH or enter retirement, you may wonder whether you have been a success in your financial planning. The first measure would be to ask, perhaps, "Do I have enough money?"

The answer is likely "yes." If you have been saving and investing following the principles of this book—whether or not you learned the principles from it—you likely have a well-funded retirement plan.

If not, you may determine that you are, in any event, a success by more meaningful definitions of the word.

Have I Done Any Good?

You know the hymn, "Have I done any Good?"[50] While the song refers to a daily assessment, a more thorough analysis of your life coinciding with your retirement may yield satisfying results. You are a success if at the point you ask the question, you can look back on your life and respond to the hymn's challenge with an unequivocal "yes." There are many areas in which you may have devoted your resources—rather than for accumulating wealth for a comfortable retirement. Consider all of the aspects of your life before you judge your retirement to be all that you hoped.

Family: President David O. McKay is famous for having advised that "No other success can compensate for failure in the home." Therefore, if you find yourself in retirement with fewer financial resources than hoped, be grateful that wise financial planning allowed you to do so much for your family. Your money may have been invested in sending children on missions or to college. You may even have suffered a financial reversal associated with helping your children out of a tough financial bind—a medical emergency, a business failure, etc. You can and should be proud of such service to your family.

Church Service: You may have hoped that your financial resources would have been sufficient to allow you to serve one or more full-time missions in retirement. If you have found, however, that your resources or your health have been depleted to the point that this will not be possible, don't despair. If you have served in the callings you've been given, you have done much for the building up of the Kingdom, already. If you desire to do more, but health or financial circumstances won't allow for full-time missionary service, the Church has a near limitless supply of service opportunities that can be matched to your available time and abilities.

While much of this book has focused on using financial resources to build up the Kingdom, it is clear that much of the Kingdom building is done by virtue of work—time spent in the Lord's employ. Time is a commodity allotted to all Saints, regardless of wealth, in equal measure every day. Brigham Young said, "Everything connected with building up Zion requires actual, severe labor. It is nonsense to talk about building up any kingdom except by labor; it requires the labor of every part of our organization, whether it be mental, physical or spiritual, and that is the only way to build up the Kingdom of God."[51]

50   Will L. Thompson, "Have I Done Any Good?" Hymns of the Church of Jesus Christ of Latter-day Saints, 1985, pp. 223.
51   Discourses of Brigham Young, p. 291.

This labor includes the things that you have done in the Church for your entire life, particularly home and visiting teaching. Sunday school lessons, primary lessons, Boy Scout campouts and enrichment activities are all a part of building the Kingdom. Having done these things, take pride in having done your part. Continue, regardless of your age, to do your part and the Lord can ask no more.

Community: You could also find yourself near retirement with fewer resources than you'd hoped to have in retirement because you rendered service in the community. Whether such service involved serving as an elected official or serving as a scoutmaster, you took the opportunity to make your part of the world a better place. By so doing, you have contributed to the welfare or wellbeing of others and you should take comfort in this.

Treasures in Heaven

The Lord Himself challenged his disciples to "lay up for yourselves treasures in heaven… for where your treasure is, there will your heart be also.[52]" If you have raised your children to the best of your ability, been true to your spouse, served in the Church or community, you have stored up treasures in heaven. Ultimately, you will retire *there*. Your eternal lifestyle will be determined by how you spent your time and money, not by how much money you accumulate. In the end, your accumulated wealth will go to your heirs, perhaps the Church will also be a beneficiary, but you cannot use this wealth to purchase a ticket that will be accepted for admission into heaven.

Rather, you'll receive admission there as a function of the grace and mercy effected by the Savior's atonement and your obedience to gospel principles. So, whether you are in retirement or in your twenties, be sure to contribute as regularly to your treasures in heaven as you do to your treasures on Earth. Don't defer Church service, righteous living, payment of tithes, having a family or community service until you have accomplished your financial goals.

Finally, therefore, consider that it is more important to do good than to do well. This should be both the foundation and capstone of your financial planning.

Action Items:

1. Measure your success by the appropriate standards—not by your balance sheet.
2. Make your family the focus of your attention.
3. Render service to church and community along the way.

---

[52]   Matthew 6:22-23

NOTE FROM THE AUTHOR

THANK YOU FOR taking the time to read *Building Wealth for Building the Kingdom*. I hope that it will bless your life, enabling you to live more comfortably while empowering you to give more and do more for the Church.

Your comments about your reaction to this book are of immeasurable help to me as I look to prepare future editions. You may send suggestions for improvement and corrections to me directly at devin@devinthorpe.com. I will respond to your email. I promise!

If you liked the book and found it helpful to you for planning your financial affairs, I would appreciate your feedback in the form of a book review at Amazon.com.

You may also wish to interact with me and other readers of the book on my blog at bw4bk.tumblr.com or on Facebook or Google +; just search for "Building Wealth for Building the Kingdom" in either place to visit my page where you can post your comments, share your experiences with saving for missions and sending your kids to college.

26594220R00081

Made in the USA
San Bernardino, CA
01 December 2015